Getting the Buggers to Write

Also available from Continuum:

Sue Cowley: *Getting the Buggers to Behave*

Sue Cowley: *Starting Teaching*

Duncan Grey: *The Internet in School*

Fred Sedgwick: *Teaching Literacy*

Getting the Buggers to Write

Sue Cowley

continuum
LONDON • NEW YORK

CONTINUUM
The Tower Building, 11 York Road, London SE1 7NX
370 Lexington Avenue, New York, NY 10017-6503

www.continuumbooks.com

First published 2002

British Library Cataloguing-in-Publication Data
A catalogue record for this book is available from the British Library.

ISBN: 0-8264-5838-6 (hardback)
      0-8264-5839-4 (paperback)

Typeset by BookEns Ltd., Royston, Herts.
Printed and bound in Great Britain by Bidddles Ltd,
Guildford and King's Lynn

Contents

Part 2: Writing across the Curriculum

Part 3: Writing it Right

Part 4: Writing: Around the Subject

Part 5: Resources for Writing

Figures

This book is dedicated to the kids in my life: Ania Giemza, Jessica, Rebecca and Elliott Castellino, Oliver Newton, Jasmine and Sébastien Charman, Luke O'Gara, Juliette Green and Big Boi.

Acknowledgements

Thanks to all the brilliant English teachers who have taught me, worked with me and inspired me, especially Miss Ladd at Burlington Danes, Hilary, Valerie and the three Johns (Osborne, Browning and Rust Andrews). Thanks to Anthony Haynes at Continuum for the great titles, and to Alexandra Webster for all her hard work on my behalf. And, of course, thanks as always to Tilak.

Introduction

Writing is fundamental: from primary to secondary school, in subjects as diverse as History, English, Science and RE, we *all* have a stake in improving our students' literacy skills. Every subject taught in schools demands that, at some point, the student must pick up a pen and make marks on paper. Or, as we move further into the technological age, that they should boot up a computer and type their thoughts on-screen. How, then, can we motivate and inspire our students to write, especially those for whom writing is a real struggle? And once we've got them writing, how can we ensure that what they produce is clear, accurate and well written?

This book aims to answer these questions. The material here will be of help to teachers working across the primary and secondary sectors, and also to those teaching post-sixteen. The ideas will be useful for English teachers, but also for teachers in all areas of the curriculum. I have included a combination of tips, teaching strategies, examples and exercises, from which you can choose those best suited to your particular needs. Although this book is packed with ideas for lessons, it is not a collection of lesson plans, nor is it a book on the theory of writing. Rather, the material here is designed to inspire you to find new and exciting ways to motivate your students to write. My own teaching experience has taught me that it is often the most unusual ideas and strategies that prove effective, especially when working with poorly motivated students.

My primary aim in this book is to offer you *practical* advice, written in an honest, accessible and straightforward way – advice that will be of immediate use to you in the classroom. The ideas included in this book are based on my own experiences as a teacher and a writer, rather than on years of painstaking theoretical research. I have tried to avoid jargon and complicated terminology, for these are the enemies of the writer and of the teacher. Our aim must always be to put across what we want to say as simply and clearly as possible, and for our students to do the same.

The National Literacy Strategy now reaches across both primary and secondary schools, and it is making teachers in all subject areas ever more aware of how crucial (and complex) the acquisition of literacy actually is. Within this book, you will find a huge range of ideas and suggestions that are linked closely to the requirements of the Literacy Strategy, especially as it concerns writing. The strategies and approaches that I give will help you teach writing in a way that will motivate and engage *all* your children, and allow you give them access to the wonderful gift of literacy.

We write for a multitude of reasons and purposes. Some students write only because they have to, while others genuinely enjoy the chance to express themselves through words. The majority of our students are involved in written communication every day of their lives, although they might not realize it, or consider it to be 'writing'. Outside class time (and sometimes even during lessons!), the sound of text messages being sent and received has become the new soundtrack of our school days. Emails and chat-rooms, too, have become the technological equivalent of the paper messages that we used to pass around amongst our peers.

The reality for teachers in the classroom starts with motivating children to turn their thoughts into words, and to present these on paper. We need to show them that writing is important, and make it clear that there is no hidden secret to good writing, simply a range of techniques that we have to learn. There is perhaps an expectation that our students should somehow 'know' how to write. They can talk, we say, so why can they not write as well? But writing is not simply about turning spoken words into written ones. It is also about learning the skills (and tricks) that help us create good writing. Just as a violin-player must learn musical technique before adding the expression that brings his or her playing to life, so we must teach our pupils the techniques that writing involves, thus giving them the freedom to express themselves both accurately and imaginatively.

Technique is not just about writing 'correctly', with the grammar, spelling and punctuation that this implies, although I do of course deal with this important area of literacy. Technique is also about learning how to structure our writing, the skills of drafting and editing, the importance of dramatic tension in telling a gripping story, how and when we can break the 'rules', and so on. In this book I will show you how you can teach all these skills in an active, interesting and exciting way to your students, and improve the writing of even the most poorly motivated children.

So, it is my hope that this book will help you in getting your students to write, and to write well. With the explosion of the internet, and technologies of all types, writing has become even *more* important, not less. By equipping our students to write well, we give them the best chance to succeed in life, to grasp all the opportunities they have to express themselves, and to contribute their ideas and thoughts to the world in whatever form of writing they choose.

Sue Cowley
www.SueCowley.co.uk

Part 1

Starting Points

1 The motivation to write

In every school, no matter how 'good' it is, there will be some students who are simply not motivated to write, or who find writing a huge challenge. You know the ones I mean: every word is a struggle, like getting blood from a stone, to use the familiar cliché. This chapter deals with different ways we can motivate and inspire our students to write, and ways that we can encourage them to keep on writing once they have started. After all, only when this initial motivation is there can we work on improving both the basics of their work, and extending their writing to a higher level.

Getting them writing

How, then, do we get our students to write? Here are some initial ideas and tips for motivating your children, which will work with all ages, and across the whole curriculum.

- *Give them a reason to write*: When we ask our students to write, our motivation as teachers might be to cover the curriculum, or to help our class pass their exams. Perhaps, though, we forget that children also need some kind of motivation for their writing. As far as possible, find ways to make the writing 'real', ways to inspire your students, to make them *want* to write. Some ideas about how you might do this are explored below, in the section 'A reason to write' (p. 8).
- *Create an atmosphere for writing*: In addition to finding this initial motivation, we should also try to create an atmosphere in which writing feels easy and natural. This could be as simple as creating a quiet and positive working environ-

ment, but it might also mean creating a 'mood' in your classroom that encourages your students to respond in a written way. Again, you can find ideas about how to do this further on in the chapter.

- *Ensure the 'correct' behaviour for writing*: If your students are misbehaving, it is likely that the atmosphere in the classroom is not conducive to good writing, or indeed to any writing. You will find some ideas below about developing focus and self-discipline. Look too at Chapter 9 for some tips on how to get and maintain good behaviour.

- *Make the writing seem like fun*: Why not make a game of writing tasks, for instance using the format of a certain popular cookery programme? Use a stopwatch and prepare your class to start with the command: 'Ready, steady, write!'

- *Use 'warm-up' exercises*: When an athlete is preparing to run, or a dancer to dance, they warm up their bodies before they begin. In the same way, we can also use 'warm-up' writing exercises to help motivate and prepare our students to write. See the section below for 'warm-up' ideas.

- *Keep it topical*: If you want to motivate your children, ask them to write about something that is of real interest to them. Utilize the latest craze (for instance, Pop Idol or Tomb Raider) as a basis for their writing. If you are choosing a text for your students to read and then write about, make sure it's something up to date and engaging. The internet is also a wonderful and topical resource for inspiring writing.

- *Work to their strengths*: Although you will obviously need to use a range of writing tasks in the classroom, do let your students write in the form or style that suits them whenever possible. A good way of doing this is to use a group 'project' where different students can work on different aspects of the task (see Chapter 6, p. 128, for more details about this).

- *Challenge them*: In my experience, students are often better motivated by work that they see as really challenging – work that you might feel is 'above' their level of ability. For instance, some pupils see English as an 'airy-fairy' subject, in contrast to the more technical demands of science or maths. Defy this assumption: teach them about extended metaphors, iambic pentameter, pathetic fallacy! The challenge of learning about these more technical aspects of the subject can be a great motivator.

- *Remove the stress*: Some of your weaker students might be fearful about writing, rather than lacking in motivation. It could be that they associate a sense of failure with the act of writing, especially if they have a specific difficulty with technique. If this is the case, on occasions tell them to write without worrying about the technical aspects of their work, such as spelling and punctuation. This will free them up: they can always go back and correct mistakes later.

- *Remove the blocks*: Similarly, some students are 'blocked' in their writing, perhaps because of a fear of failure or of 'getting it wrong'. If this is the case, try using the 'stream of consciousness' technique to free up their writing. See the section 'Warm-up exercises' in this chapter (p. 12) for an explanation of this idea.

- *Offer a reward*: We all work best when there is a carrot ahead of us, rather than a stick behind us. Work out exactly what will best motivate your students in their writing, whether this is stickers, merits or Mars bars. Have high expectations of what your children can or will achieve, and then reward them when their work really deserves it.

- *Show that writing is relevant*: Talk to your children about the role of writing in their own lives: text messages, emails, the internet, magazines, and so on. Use these contemporary forms of writing as a resource to inspire your students.

- *Show that writing is important*: Talk to your classes about why writing is important, offering your own ideas and asking your students about their feelings. Talk with them about how we write to communicate, for pleasure and self-expression, to remember things, to pass exams, and so on.

- *Show yourself as a writer*: Your students should see you writing as much as possible: on a blackboard or whiteboard, on an OHP, on their work. See the section 'Teacher as writer' later on in this chapter (p. 16) for some more ideas on this.

- *Offer yourself as an inspiration*: It is the teachers who were most passionate about their subjects and their teaching that I remember from my schooldays, the ones with that indefinable 'spark'. Sometimes we get bogged down in the minutiae of the daily grind, and forget that we have the ability to inspire our children. If you show your students how much you love writing, and how excited you are about the work that they produce, then you could have the reward of inspiring them for life.

Keeping them writing

Once motivated, students will often start to write with enthusiasm, but then run out of steam halfway through an extended piece of work. Here are some tips for keeping that motivation to write going once you have got them underway.

- *Set them 'amount' targets*: Ask them to write a specific amount, i.e. half a page or 50 words. For an individual who is experiencing particular difficulties, you could put a mark on the page and ask them to write down to this point.
- *Set them 'time' targets*: Writing for a long period of time can be counterproductive. Enthusiasm flags, exhaustion sets in, and the quality of the writing becomes poor. Set your students a certain length of time for their writing: fifteen minutes is about right for them to retain their focus and energy.
- *Keep it fresh*: Give your students regular breaks when they are writing: for instance, after writing for fifteen minutes, they could take a five-minute break to refresh themselves. This time could be used to discuss samples of the work so far, or simply for the students to chat with a partner about their writing.
- *Develop their concentration*: A good level of concentration is necessary when writing, especially if you have to write for any length of time (for instance, in an exam). This self-discipline and focus is something that many students seem to lack. You can find ideas for developing concentration further on in this chapter, in the section on 'Focus exercises' (p. 14).
- *Give them a test*: You've probably noticed how, as exam time approaches, your students become much more focused in their work. Many teachers offer their classes 'exam practice' in the run-up to national tests and exams, but there is no need to

restrict tests to these times alone. In addition, a test offers the teacher a chance for a 'lesson off', although you should stagger the setting of tests to allow for the additional marking load. And of course, not all tests need to be marked by the teacher. See Chapter 7 for more ideas about setting and marking tests and exams.

- *Use unusual motivators*: In my experience, students are always motivated by unusual or imaginative resources or teaching strategies. When approaching work on the Shakespeare play *Romeo and Juliet*, an excellent motivator I have used is to set up the story as a crime-scene investigation. The students then work as police officers to examine the evidence and interview witnesses.

Getting them writing properly

As well as having to deal with students who won't write at all, you will also encounter those who produce pages and pages of writing, but whose work is illegible, or has no punctuation, or doesn't make any sense. So, in addition to getting our students writing, and keeping them at it, we also need to find ways of ensuring that what they write is meaningful and worthwhile. Here are some thoughts about how you might do this.

- *Show them why writing properly is important*: In order to communicate with an audience, our writing must be legible, clear and accurate. Demonstrate this to your class by using the following exercise. Give your students a few moments to write down a short message, but with the wrong hand (i.e. the right-handed students write with their left hands, and vice versa). When they have finished, ask them to swap with a partner for translation, and discuss the difficulties of reading and understanding.
- *Show them examples of 'incorrect' writing*: By looking at a piece of writing that is 'incorrect', students will see the difficulties this creates for the reader. One way of doing this is to take a section of text and then tippex out all the punctuation. By studying the result, your students will see how difficult it is to read when the correct punctuation has not been used.

More ideas for working on punctuation skills are given in Chapter 2.

- *Share the work with the class*: In my experience, many students never get a chance to see their classmates' writing. Encourage your students to share, and even to mark, each other's work. If students know that their peers will be reading a piece of writing, they are likely to take care over it. In addition, students will start to get a sense of the type and quality of work that others are producing. (Do, however, be careful not to demotivate the very weakest students when using this technique.)

- *Share the work across the school*: In addition to sharing writing within a class group, there is no reason at all why you shouldn't share writing across year groups. This would work well in both the primary and the secondary school, for instance asking your students to write letters to their younger school mates.

- *Ask them to read their writing back to you*: Some weaker writers will finish a piece of work quickly, but will not bother to read it through (perhaps for fear of what they might see!). When students bring you pieces of writing that are illegible, or that lack punctuation, ask them to read their work back to you. The ensuing struggle should help them to realize the vital importance of writing 'properly'.

A reason to write

The majority of writing done in school is guided by the teacher: 'I want you to write a newspaper report based on the story we've been reading'; 'I'd like you all to write up this science experiment for homework.' The piece of writing produced is then judged by the teacher and graded accordingly. Obviously this is necessary if we are to fulfil curriculum requirements and assess our students. However, it does mean that writing can come to seem like a chore and not a choice, something that students must do but without any real motivation. Here, then, are some ideas for giving your students 'a reason to write'.

- *Relate the writing to their own lives*: Many students now use text-messaging on their mobile phones on a daily (or even hourly) basis. If they see how their own communication needs the skill of writing, they are far more likely to be motivated for other writing tasks you set them. Text messages also offer a very interesting insight into the way that language develops and adapts to suit its medium. Here is an exercise that you could use to help motivate your students, using text-messaging. Write the following text message on the board and ask your class to translate it.

  RUOK? Y R U ☹? PCM. D8 2NITE? BCNU L8R.

  (If you're not 'txt liter8' see Appendix 1 which deals with text-messaging to find out what this says.) You could then move into a discussion about how and why languages change and develop. Alternatively, you could ask your students to write a story using text-message abbreviations. In Appendix 2 you will find information about an exciting project called 'the-phone-book.com' that combines story-writing and text messaging.

- *Make the writing fun*: It is sometimes hard to think up ways to make writing 'fun', whilst at the same time retaining its educational value. Try to think laterally – how could I approach this task in an unusual, humorous or imaginative way? For instance, some teachers ask their students to 'write about yourself' as an introductory piece of writing. A lateral way to approach this task would be to ask your students to write their own obituary (perhaps including details of the horrific way in which they died). Whilst this may seem rather gruesome, it certainly captures the attention and offers an unusual way into a familiar topic.

- *Give them an inspiration to write*: Unusual or imaginative resources or ideas can prove compelling to students. The same, too, applies to finding sources of inspiration. Creating a 'fiction' of some type can prove very inspirational. For instance, young children might bring in a favourite toy to school, and be asked to interview their toy. They could then write the story that their doll or teddy tells them. Older children respond well to an inspiration that puts them in a position of authority. For instance, the idea that they are 'television executives' writing a documentary or drama on a specific topic.

- *Make the writing 'real'*: Writing at school can often be rather contrived. For it to give maximum pleasure, it needs to feel real, to have a genuine reason for taking place. Encourage your students to use writing for a 'real' purpose, to express their thoughts or communicate their opinions. For instance, they could write an email or letter to an author whose work they love. Alternatively, they could write to a local or national newspaper to complain about an issue of import-ance to them. In addition to giving a sense of purpose, they may well receive replies to their letters, which will give them added encouragement and motivation.

- *Use a group project*: Group projects allow each student more of a choice in the form and style of writing they are going to do, depending on their strengths or interests. In addition, by offering a fairly wide selection of subjects, each group can make a choice based on personal enjoyment of a particular topic. (See Chapter 6 for more thoughts about group projects.)

- *Set up a competition*: A whole-school writing competition can prove a wonderful motivator for student writing. I had fun with this idea in my first year of teaching, when I set up a whole-school poetry competition. You could choose one style of writing, such as poetry, or allow a range of genres. This idea would work well in many areas of the curriculum, for instance a competition for the best history or science project, or for the best biography of a well-known sports-man or woman in PE. Your school or department might be able to fund small prizes to reward the winners, for instance book tokens. If you publish the winning and commended entries in a book or pamphlet, this will celebrate the students' achievements and make them feel like 'real' writers.

An atmosphere for writing

Setting an atmosphere for writing is all about creating a 'mood' in your classroom in which writing takes place naturally. It could be that the mood you create helps to inspire your students, or it might be that it simply provides a quiet, positive place in which to work. Here are some ideas for creating an atmosphere for writing.

- *Set the boundaries for written work*: Right from the start, set your boundaries for how written work takes place. You may believe that writing should always be done in silence, or you may feel that a low level of talk is acceptable. Perhaps your students write best when listening to music. Talk to your classes about their preferred atmosphere for written work, negotiating the boundaries with them. If some of your older students genuinely work best when listening to music, you might feel that allowing them to use a walkman whilst writing is acceptable, although I would only make this offer to GCSE groups and above.
- *Think about your classroom set-up*: Try to create a 'comfort zone' for writing, an environment in which external factors do not interfere with the writing process. Ensure, as far as possible, that your students have room on their desks and are not constantly banging elbows with the person sitting next to them. Think, too, about the levels of heat and light in your room, and how these might adversely affect your children's writing.
- *Create a dramatic atmosphere*: An inspiring or dramatic atmosphere for writing can really help to motivate your students. You might set the mood for writing a ghost-story by blacking out the classroom and sharing some ghost-stories with your class by torchlight, before the writing begins. To develop this idea, you could play a soundtrack of howling wind and creepy night creatures.
- *Use a variety of inspirations*: Again, think about unusual resources for inspiration: music, pictures, objects, etc. can all help create an atmosphere for writing. I have always found that bringing in a prop of some sort helps to inspire my students and engage their interest in the lesson. For instance,

you might bring in a 'magical' box, and tell your students that it is locked shut, and cannot be opened (except by the right spell, of course!). The children could then write about what they imagine might be inside the box, and what the spell is that opens it.

Warm-up exercises

Just as pianists might play some scales to warm up their fingers, or dancers do some stretches to warm up their bodies, so writers need to 'warm up' before they begin to work. The warm-ups described below cover both the physical and mental aspects of writing.

- *Finger exercises*: Some people suffer from cramp in their hands when writing for long periods of time. This may be the result of a poor writing technique, or of tension within the hands. You can help your students overcome this by using physical warm-ups before you start written work. These finger exercises are also fun! Here is just one example, but there are plenty more that you can do (any pianists at your school will be able to advise you). Ask your children to raise their hands in the air, palms away from their bodies. Now tell them to clench their fists tight, then spread their fingers as wide as possible, feeling the stretch in their palms. Repeat this several times.
- *Brainstorming*: Many teachers use a brainstorm to begin a topic as a matter of course, and this technique does provide an excellent intellectual warm-up activity. By gathering together your students' ideas and noting them on the board, you can develop confidence in the less able, by giving them some ideas to include in their writing. You will also help the more able to exercise their brains and decide exactly what they already know. Brainstorming is also a vital technique when planning longer pieces of writing such as essays.
- *Stream of consciousness*: Our minds are often full of background chatter, thoughts and feelings that may or may not be useful in our writing, but which usually get in the way. The stream of consciousness technique allows your students

to 'tip out' the 'trash can' of thoughts that are in their heads, to see what is in there, and it also helps them free up their writing. Set a time for this exercise – about two or three minutes is enough. When you say 'go' the students start writing, and they must keep going until you say 'stop'. They could write on a specific topic, or just write down any words or thoughts that come into their heads. If they get stuck, they should just keep writing the same word over and over again until they become 'unstuck'. There is no need to include any punctuation, nor to worry about spelling.

- *Narrowing the focus*: This provides a good follow-up exercise to the stream of consciousness. It is also useful for getting your students to look at their writing and to consider which words are more valuable or interesting than others. When the children have finished writing their stream of consciousness, ask them to count the number of words on the page. They must then cut this number exactly in half, crossing out any words that seem irrelevant or unimportant. The writing does not need to make sense. When they have finished the first cut, ask them to cut the number in half again, so that they end up with exactly a quarter of the original word-count. If you wish, you could follow this up by asking them to use the remaining words to create a poem. They could be allowed to swap or barter words with other students in the class.

- *Collaborative writing*: This is a fun way to warm up for a story-writing activity. Ask each student to take a single sheet of paper and to write the first sentence of a story on the top line. When they have done this, they pass the paper on to the next student, who writes the next line of the story, then folds the paper down so that only the sentence that they have written is visible. Some of the collaborative stories written in this way can be very amusing. The sense of this being a collaborative activity also takes some of the fear out of writing a story for those students who are less confident about their work.

- *Picturing a story*: Again, this provides a good warm-up to a story-writing activity, although it could be adapted to suit other forms of writing. In addition, it provides a useful technique for students who tend to 'dive into' their writing without thinking about it first. Ask your students to close their eyes and to picture the story in their heads, as though they are running a film. The teacher could tell them a story, or they could come up with ideas of their own, perhaps based on a particular topic.

Focus exercises

The following 'focus exercises' are all about developing the vital skills of self-discipline and concentration. They provide good warm-ups for a writing session and help you to get your students in the mood for any piece of work that requires extended concentration. They are based on drama exercises, but should prove suitable for teachers in any subject who wish to develop their students' concentration skills. Some need an open space, while others can be used in a normal classroom setting. These focus exercises are, in my experience, extremely popular with children of all ages. (During my teaching career I have used them with students aged three to eighteen!)

- *Hypnosis*: This exercise requires the students to focus on one thing for a length of time – the basic requirement for concentration. Demonstrate the exercise first by asking a student to come to the front of the class to be 'hypnotized' by you. Tell the student that when you click your fingers they will be 'under your power'. Hold your palm up so that it is level with their face, a short distance away. Once the student is 'under your power', they must follow you wherever you go, keeping their face at exactly the same distance from your hand. Move your hand around slowly, up and down, side to side, down to the floor, and so on. If you are brave enough, after demonstrating the exercise you can let the volunteer hypnotize you in return. This exercise could then be done by the whole class, working in pairs.
- *Count down*: Again, this exercise helps set a 'focus' for your students. They should shut their eyes, and then count backwards from 50 to zero. When they reach zero, they can open their eyes and prepare to work.

- *Mental spelling*: Along the same lines as the exercise above, this activity also helps develop concentration and focus. Ask your students to close their eyes, and then spell a word or words backwards in their heads. For instance, you could start by asking them to spell their full names.
- *Listening*: This is a very simple exercise, useful for setting a calm atmosphere before writing begins. Ask your children to close their eyes and simply listen to see what they can hear. At first, they could focus on sounds within the classroom, gradually moving out to sounds in the corridors, and around the school.
- *Puppets*: This drama exercise not only develops concentration but also the skills of cooperation and coordination. Again, you could demonstrate it using a student volunteer. One person is the 'puppet-master', the other the puppet. The puppet-master moves their puppet around through the use of invisible strings, keeping their hand at a short distance from the part of the body they are moving. The strings can be attached to the hands, feet, elbows and knees. Alternatively, for an even higher level of focus, there could be strings on each of the fingers, on the head, and so on.

Putting the pleasure back into writing

As we have seen, the contrived nature of much writing in schools means that our students learn to see writing as part of the toil of the school day, rather than something that they might choose to do. We need to show them that it is possible to gain pleasure from writing, or to use it as a way to express themselves. Here are some ideas about how you might do this.

- *Have a 'free writing' session*: On occasions, perhaps once a fortnight, give your students the chance to write purely for pleasure. Offer them a totally free choice of form and style: they can write about whatever they want, in any style or form they wish. Tell them that for this session technique is unimportant – you are not going to be judging or assessing what they write. Some students might choose to write notes to each other, others to write an article about their favourite pop group. Rather than marking their writing, ask your class to share their work by reading it out loud. Talk to them about their reasons for choosing a particular form and subject and why it appeals to them. In this way you will also learn more about your students' interests – information that you can put to use in planning your lessons.

- *Offer valuable rewards for good writing*: Depending on what motivates your students, whether it is merit marks or Mars bars, use these rewards to encourage good writing. In addition, the reward of seeing their work published can be a huge factor in giving your students pleasure from writing. There are many websites that publish student work (see Appendix 2 for some examples), or you could set up your own page on a school website to 'show off' the best writing.
- *Display good written work*: Displaying good pieces of writing will help motivate your students, both those whose work is on display and those who look at the displays. Remember to display the work of your less able as well as your more able students. If you feel it is necessary, redraft or type up a piece of work to correct spelling errors before displaying it.
- *Encourage keen writers*: There are probably students in your class who write for pleasure outside school time, although you may not be aware of it. I have been approached by my own students with examples of poetry, novels, auto-biographies, letters and so on. 'Could you read this for me, miss?' they ask, and I am always happy to oblige. Show your students that you are interested in any writing that they do, not just in the class assignments that you set.

The teacher as writer

Seeing their teacher as a writer is an excellent way of motivating students, and it will also help them learn about the processes involved in writing. Your students see you as a writer when you scribble notes on the classroom blackboard or whiteboard; when you teach them using an overhead projector or an electronic whiteboard; when you write comments on their work, praising what is good and suggesting how their writing might be improved. Here are some ideas about the teacher as writer that you may find useful.

- *Articulate the process*: When teaching your class through your own writing, you have the opportunity to show that writing is an active process, one in which decisions are constantly being made. Comment on your own writing as it takes place. As you write, talk about the thoughts that go through your head: how should I structure this, where should I put that idea, which words should I use?
- *Involve your students*: As you work on a piece of writing, ask for your students' ideas, involving them in the act of decision-making. Allow your students to contribute to the process, either orally or by coming up to the board and writing down their ideas.
- *Create a dialogue*: Another good idea is to use writing to set up a dialogue with your students. For instance, you might write a series of questions on a piece of completed writing, and ask the student to reply to your queries. In this way, they will learn more about the reviewing and editing process: how we decide what works well and how we change what could work better. Another tip is to write a letter to each of your students about their writing and about targets for improvement. They could answer your letter, setting some additional targets of their own.
- *Use examples of teachers' writing*: As well as showing yourself as a writer, you could also show examples of other teachers' writing. An idea about how you might do this can be found in the next chapter, in the section entitled 'Graphology' (p. 37).

2 The basics

The basics of language are the tools of the writer, just as a set of different coloured paints and a selection of brushes are the tools of the painter. Whilst students can express themselves reasonably well without getting the basics completely right, their writing will never be as good as it might be if they are not technically accurate (and of course they won't get such good grades in their exams!). This chapter offers you some thoughts and ideas for getting the basics right. These are not 'lessons' as such, but rather some different approaches and strategies for dealing with the basics of writing.

Traditionally, the job of teaching 'the basics' has taken place during 'English lessons' at primary level, or has fallen to English teachers in secondary schools. However, the Literacy Strategy asks that *all* teachers take a stake in teaching good writing skills, and this is surely an approach to be welcomed. After all, good literacy allows our children access to all areas of the curriculum through the written word. Without these skills, our students will be impeded when they leave school, not just in their career prospects but in every area of their lives. In my experience, teachers are naturally good at working as a team, and ensuring that 'the basics' are monitored across all curriculum areas is one very positive aspect of this teamwork.

Spelling

Just as when motivating your students to write, if you want them to spell correctly, they must understand why this is important. Talk to them about why we need accurate spelling for good writing.

- *Communication*: Getting our spelling right enables us to communicate effectively – a common way of spelling is almost as important as a common language for proper communication.
- *Accuracy*: Spelling properly means that our writing is 'correct' and accurate. Just as a chemist would mix up the proper ingredients for an experiment, so we must incorporate the correct ingredients into our writing. Of course, spelling is not just a matter of writing correctly in English lessons, it is also about learning to spell key terms across the curriculum.
- *Hiding the technique*: The secret of really good writing is to ensure that nothing intervenes between the reader and what they are reading, that the technique is completely hidden. For instance, a skilled story-writer will immerse the audience totally in the fiction, until the reader feels as though the normal world has disappeared, and only the story world exists. If the reader notices spelling mistakes (or any other aspect of poor technique), then this will distract them from being absorbed in the writing itself.
- *Exam success*: The ability to spell properly allows us to succeed in our exams. Whatever the rights and wrongs of an emphasis on correct spelling, we (and our students) must accept that accurate spelling will indeed gain them better results. Be honest with your students – show them the marking criteria that apply to this area and explain exactly how their results will be affected by a poor standard of spelling.

Spelling difficulties

Problems with spelling can occur for a number of reasons, and it is well worth the teacher (of whatever age or subject) being aware of why errors occur. After all, only by identifying the root cause of the difficulty can we put the relevant strategies for correcting spelling into place. Here are some of the reasons why errors may occur. You can find some suggested solutions to these difficulties in the following sections.

- *Special learning needs*: In some cases, for instance the student with dyslexia, the errors are a result of a specific difficulty. You can find some useful organizations involved in helping children with particular learning needs in Appendix 2.

- *A phonic approach to language*: Children who have learned to read with a strongly or solely phonic approach may try to spell words as they sound. This is fine for the phonic words in our language, but many words in English are not spelt in the same way that they are said.
- *A 'real books' approach to language*: Similarly, children who have learned to read without any phonic input will find it hard to 'sound out' words, and to work out their spelling in this way. Happily, the majority of schools now use a range of approaches when teaching reading.
- *A lack of reading experience*: Constant exposure to words through reading will inevitably help with spelling. After all, if we have seen a word spelt correctly hundreds or thousands of times, we develop a visual memory of the correct spelling of that word. The child who has little interest in reading, or who finds it a struggle, will have 'met' less words than the keen reader, and will consequently find spelling harder.
- *A lack of spelling strategies*: Some students may never have been taught any strategies for learning and remembering spellings. By teaching them these strategies we will not only help them improve their spelling but also encourage them to look at the roots and structure of language itself.
- *Laziness*: Let's be honest: some children can't be bothered to check their work through for errors, or simply are not motivated to care enough about their writing to ensure that their spelling is correct.

Dealing with spelling difficulties

How, then, do we help our students when they do have spelling difficulties? With the traditional method of rote-learning, and the weekly spelling test, our children may well learn to spell the list of words that we give them. However, this type of memorizing is generally very short-lived, and without the strategies to retain the learning it is really pretty meaningless. Perhaps one of the most useful things that we can do is to encourage our children to develop their own strategies for learning how to spell. Here are a range of tips and ideas that you may find helpful when dealing with your own students' spelling difficulties.

- *Study the words*: Digging deeply into the language they use will encourage your children to find ways of learning and remembering spellings. For instance, they could be taught to divide words up into syllables, or to search for the linguistic roots of words that are new to them. The section 'Top tips for learning spellings' (p. 23) gives you ideas about how to study words in depth.

- *Use visual aids*: Do ensure that you label the 'things' in your classroom. Many primary teachers will do this naturally to help with literacy skills. However, secondary teachers tend to overlook this useful technique, which can aid spelling across the curriculum.

- *Use visual memory tricks*: In addition to labelling your resources and the parts of your room, use visual ways of remembering words. For instance, a primary teacher working on the word 'bed' could tell their children to make a 'bed' with their fingers to spell the word. In this way, the children learn to put the 'b' and 'd' the correct way around.

- *Look at the shape of words*: Ask your children to explore the shape of the words that they are trying to spell. By exploring which parts of the words are tall or short, or which come under or over the lines on a page, you can help them in memorizing the visual appearance of a word.

- *Find rhyming word families*: By connecting 'families' of rhyming words that are relatively easy to spell, children will find it easier to understand and remember the vocabulary. At the simplest level, this might mean looking at 'at' words, such as cat, hat and mat. At a later stage in their schooling, you might use longer rhyming words, such as chance, advance and enhance.

- *Use imaginative resources*: In my experience, children (and indeed adults) are inspired to learn by an imaginative, engaging approach. Using 'props' is a relatively easy way of sparking interest, for instance creating a display of science equipment, and giving volunteers the 'reward' of holding or using the equipment as the rest of the class learn the spellings.

- *Adopt unusual approaches*: Similarly, an unusual or lateral approach to spelling tasks can be very engaging. For instance, give your students a passage in which all the words are spelt phonetically rather than accurately. The strange appearance of such a passage will make the point very clearly that English is not a completely phonetic language.

- *Use spell-checkers*: Using the spell-checker on a computer can be helpful when dealing with spelling difficulties, especially for children who are making only small errors in their writing. After all, why not use all the technology that we have at our disposal? However, there are limitations to the usefulness of spell-checkers. If the child's spelling is very poor, the computer may not be able to 'work out' the word that they are actually trying to spell. In addition, spell-checkers cannot help the uncertain speller with homophones. There is also the danger that the child comes to rely on the spell-checker, rather than using his or her own strategies to learn new words. To avoid this, you could get the student to list all the words that are picked out by the computer as being incorrectly spelt. These words could then be added to a 'bank' of spellings that the child must memorize.

- *Use dictionaries*: As well as encouraging the use of dictionaries, do ensure that you teach your children how to use them! As adults, we tend to assume that using a dictionary is straightforward, but it is in fact a skill that needs to be taught. You can find some more ideas about using dictionaries in the section 'Working with words' (p. 40) later on in this chapter.

- *Create a sense of 'ownership'*: If we feel that we 'own' our learning, that it belongs to us in a personal way, we tend to take it more seriously. To put this idea into practice, you might get your students to create their own lists of spellings to learn, ones that they personally find particularly difficult. Alternatively, you could fill a box with some of the most commonly used words, and get your children to pick out the ones that they must learn.

- *Supply the vocabulary*: The Literacy Strategy asks us to put a strong focus on learning new words and key terms across the curriculum. When first approaching a new topic area, for instance letter-writing or graphic design, make sure you supply your students with the words they will need. You can find cross-curricular lists of useful vocabulary in Appendix 3.

- *Set regular tests*: The Literacy Strategy also encourages us to use a 'starter activity' in our lessons. By using this time to set spellings, and to give strategies for learning and remembering them, your children will gradually develop a 'bank' of accurate spellings for your subject. Whatever the pros and cons of spelling tests, they do offer a useful way of analysing exactly where your children's weaknesses lie, and which words prove particularly difficult for individual students.

- *Research your children's special needs*: If you have a child with a special need in your class, do try to find some time to research the area in question. Innovative new ideas are constantly being developed for dealing with special needs such as dyslexia. There are some website addresses for finding information about special needs in Appendix 2.

- *Encourage them to read*: As I have said, the repeated exposure to vocabulary that takes place during reading will inevitably have an impact on spelling. Make the connection completely transparent to your children – let them know that the most active readers will generally be the most successful spellers and writers.

Top tips for learning spellings

The following tips will help students who find it difficult to learn spellings, but they are also very useful for any child attempting to learn a new word. By looking at words in this sort of detail, our students begin to understand the mechanics of the English language, just as they might learn about the mechanics of addition in a maths lesson.

- *Relationships*: Relate the word being learned to another word your students already know. This gives the children a 'hook' on which they can 'hang' the word they are memorizing. (For instance, the word 'obedient' relates to 'obey', the word 'prejudice' to 'prejudge'.) A useful idea for developing this exercise is to ask your children to make a list of all words that are similar to a new spelling. They could do this by searching through a dictionary, or simply by brainstorming their ideas.

- *Find the words within a word*: Looking inside a word, to find out what else is there, can be a good way of exploring the logic of spelling. For instance, within the word 'courageous' we find the word 'courage', although the sound of the word is slightly different.

- *Split words into syllables*: Splitting a word up into its separate sounds will help your students to remember a spelling. For example, splitting 'February' up into 'Feb/ru/ary', or 'particularly' into 'par/tic/u/lar/ly'.

- *Unusual sounds*: Carrying on from the idea above, many words in English are not spelt phonically (as we say them), or they have a 'hidden' sound within them. With these words, tell your students to emphasize the difficult part of the word in their heads, but as spelt, rather than said, correctly. For instance, in the two examples above, the 'ru' sound in February would be emphasized, as would the 'lar' sound in particularly.

- *Memory links*: Links can be formed between certain words and their spelling. For instance, to remember the word 'exaggerate' talk about the fact that it has two 'g's rather than one. This ties in with the whole idea of exaggerating! Similarly, the word 'too' means very and has more than one 'o'.

- *Learn letter combinations and sounds*: Certain letter combinations are common in English, and once their spelling is learned, they help children access and spell a wide range of related words. (For instance, the sound 'tion' at the end of competition, action, and so on. Similarly, the combination 'tious' at the end of superstitious, ambitious, etc).

- *Use the roots of language*: Referring your students to the etymology of the words they use will help them see the logic behind non-phonetic spellings. (For instance, the word 'beautiful' begins with the word 'beau', taken from the French. If we were to spell the word phonetically, it would be something like 'bewteafull'!) Look for patterns within different subject terminology and explore where these words or letter combinations came from. This could lead to some fascinating work on the historical origins of different curriculum subjects.

- *Study Greek and Latin roots*: In addition to exploring words that come from another language, learning about Greek and Latin prefixes and suffixes can be very helpful. For instance, the prefix 'hypo' in 'hypocritical' and 'hypodermic', or the letter combination 'psy' in 'psychiatrist' and 'psychology'.
- *Picture the words*: As we have already seen, the best readers are often very good at spelling too. They are able to 'see' a word and know whether it is right or wrong because they have seen it many times in their reading. Encourage your students to visualize words in their heads as spelt correctly. An extension of this is when a child always spells the same word wrongly. Tell him to picture the wrong spelling in his head, with a huge red cross through it.
- *Learn the rules*: I have put this idea at the end of my 'top tips', because in my experience, unless a 'rule' is especially memorable, children tend to forget them. In addition, some of the spelling rules we ask our students to learn are very complicated. A rule that has stayed with me from school (and probably with many of you, as well) is 'i before e, except after c'. We remember this rule because it rhymes, and this shows the importance of making spelling strategies memorable. However, even with this rule there is a complication. The rule in full is, in fact, 'words with an "e" sound have i before e, except after c'.

Some thoughts on homophones

Homophones or homonyms (words that sound the same, but are spelt differently) can prove a particular challenge for students (and sometimes for their teachers too). As we saw above, links between the meaning of words and their spelling can be especially easy to remember. In addition, the more unusual or 'wacky' the idea is, the more memorable it will be. The following list gives just a few examples.

- *Here and hear*: This homophone is easy, because the word 'hear' has an 'ear' in it. Emphasize the point by asking your children to put their hand behind one ear and call out 'I h *ear* you!'

- *There and their*: Similarly, the word 'their' has an 'i' in it, and this can be related to the fact that it means 'belonging to'. Tell your students to remember that when they own something, they would say 'I own it.' This will help them to remember the 'i' in the word.
- *Words with 'ere'*: Words with 'ere' in them tend to be words related to place, e.g. here, there, where. You might help your students remember this by using the phrase 'come over 'ere'.

Punctuation

As we have seen with spelling, the first priority when dealing with punctuation is to explain to our students exactly *why* it is so important to punctuate correctly. The four areas that we identified for spelling apply equally to punctuation: we need to punctuate our writing properly so that we can communicate effectively; so that our writing is 'correct' and accurate; so that the reader can focus on *what* we are saying, rather than how we are saying it; and so that we can succeed in our studies and get the best possible results in our exams. In addition to these reasons, punctuation is also vital for finding a 'voice' in our writing, and for expressing ourselves in the tone that we want our audience to hear.

one of the best ways to explore the need for correct punctuation is to show your students a piece of writing with all the punctuation removed ask them to try to read the writing out loud the difficulties that they experience in doing this will help show the importance of punctuating properly in addition the weird experience of reading a paragraph that has no full stops commas speech marks or capital letters will help to emphasize how important punctuation is as we have seen a strange or unusual approach will often stick in the minds of your children im willing to bet that this paragraph has grabbed your attention

Problems with punctuation
Problems with punctuating correctly can occur for a variety of reasons, and again it is well worth the teacher understanding the possible source of the students' difficulties.

- *Lack of understanding*: Some children simply don't appear to understand how and when different types of punctuation mark should be used. It may be that they have not been taught the 'rules' of punctuation early on, or because they have forgotten them, or because they simply cannot be bothered!

- *Lack of experience*: A lack of understanding can also stem from inexperience in dealing with the use of punctuation. This may be because a child is new to reading, or because they have had little previous experience of books and writing.

- *Overenthusiasm*: When we are enthusiastic about our writing it is all too easy to get carried away and write reams and reams but to forget to punctuate it. The ideas rush into your head, one after the other, and you are desperate to get them down on paper before you forget them. Alternatively, an overenthusiastic writer might make excessive use of exclamation marks – a weakness I must confess that I suffer from!

- *The 'and' disease*: Carrying on from the idea above, some children use the word 'and' as an alternative to dividing their work up into sentences. Again, this may be a result of over-enthusiasm, or perhaps because they do not know of other connectives and conjunctions to use in their writing.

- *Laziness*: Again, let's be honest: some of our students are not sufficiently motivated to check their work through for accuracy. You'll find some ideas below about how you might encourage them to do this. The ideal, however, is always for students to punctuate *as they write*, rather than as an afterthought.

Dealing with punctuation problems

Here are some ideas and approaches for helping those students who experience problems with their punctuation. These strategies should be helpful at all ages where children are experiencing difficulties.

- *Explain the logic of punctuation*: Talk to your children about how punctuation helps us structure our writing. Show them how commas and full stops offer a chance to take a 'breath' when reading (either in their heads or out loud). Explore the way that a list of items is separated by the use of commas, and so on.

- *Revisit the rules*: Whatever age of children you teach, it is always worth revisiting the rules of punctuation. It could be that you need to explore the use of colons and semicolons with GCSE students, or that you need to revisit the rules about commas with Year 6 children. This would fit well with some grammar work, for instance on sentence structure.
- *Read it back*: Asking a child to read back their writing, either to you or to another student, will force them to consider the need for punctuation. If they have completed a piece of writing without any full stops, the difficulties they experience in reading it back will emphasize the need for punctuation to communicate effectively.
- *Set targets*: For the child who experiences severe difficulties in punctuating, a simple target such as 'put a full stop at the end of every sentence' could be set.
- *Encourage punctuating while writing*: There is always the temptation for students to 'go back' and add in punctuation, rather than punctuating as they write. However, this approach reinforces the weakness, and it is also a dangerous approach come exam time. Instead, try to encourage your children to punctuate each sentence as it is written, perhaps using the technique below.
- *Encourage the mental formation of sentences*: To help with the problem above, encourage your students to form each sentence in their head (or out loud) before writing it down. This technique also helps with the skills of focus and concentration.
- *Develop the use of conjunctions and connectives*: As we noted above, the 'and' disease can be a result of a lack of knowledge of different connectives. You could brainstorm a series of connecting words or phrases to use in a particular piece of writing, or alternatively provide a list of 'sentence-starters' that give your children a frame to use in their work. For instance, their first sentence could start with 'At first', their second with 'Next', their third with 'However', and so on.

- *Make punctuation fun*: Punctuation can be a rather 'dry' subject, so do try to approach it in an interesting or lateral way. For instance, you might 'sell' your children a card with a certain number of full stops, commas and exclamation marks on it, and tell them that they must use up their whole allocation of punctuation in a piece of writing. Alternatively, you could have a 'punctuation box' that the children can go to, to pull out 'their' punctuation. This idea again encourages ownership of the learning.
- *Use 'cut and paste' activities*: This is an idea I have used to great effect. Pick a suitable passage and then go through it, tippexing out all the punctuation, writing down each piece of punctuation you cut out at the bottom of the page. Now ask your students to cut and paste in the 'missing' punctuation, ensuring that they use up every full stop, speechmark, etc.

Some thoughts on apostrophes

When trying to punctuate, apostrophes do seem to cause particular problems for some of our students. Again, approach this problem by explaining the logic of the apostrophe: that it replaces a letter that is missing, or that it indicates ownership.

Here are two exercises that deal specifically with apostrophes.

- *The missing letter*: To demonstrate this rule, ask your students to write out the word in full. For instance, 'it is' or 'they are'. Now tell them to cross out the 'missing letter' (preferably with a big red cross, so that the exercise is memorable) and then replace it with an apostrophe.
- *Belonging*: This way of putting apostrophes in the correct place is one that I still remember from my own schooldays. When trying to work out where to put an apostrophe, for example in the phrase 'the childrens books', turn the phrase around so that it says 'the books *belonging to* the children'. Then the apostrophe simply goes at the end of 'children', before the 's'.

Grammar

When teaching 'grammar' as a discrete subject, we need to be careful to keep the topic as interesting and engaging as possible, especially when we are trying to motivate reluctant writers. Direct teaching of grammar has the potential to be rather dry, likely to demotivate those we most need to encourage. In addition to this, some of the rules of English grammar are complex and difficult to understand. In this section you will find some ideas about how to motivate your students in learning about grammar, and how to teach the topic in an exciting and original way. You will also find some tips on an 'active approach' to grammar: getting students to work with their own writing, and with other texts, looking at the way in which words are used, the effects they create and how they might be changed. As part of this active approach, teachers can start to introduce grammatical terminology as a natural part of working with language.

Problems with grammar
When we are babies learning a language as our 'mother tongue', we don't sit down and study the rules of grammar with our parents. Instead, the rules are internalized through the process of actually speaking the language, of using and hearing it on a daily basis. Knowledge about grammar, and grammatical terminology, might come about as a result of learning a foreign language, the grammatical rules of which may be very different to those of English. For this reason, children who have been brought up in an environment where little Standard English is spoken may encounter difficulties with writing grammatically correct English. There can be a tendency for them to translate their speaking into writing, for instance, putting 'could of' instead of 'could have'. This problem highlights the importance of speaking and listening work, focusing on the use of Standard English.

Direct teaching of grammar
In the first chapter of this book, I pointed out that students can be motivated by work that they see as a real challenge. There is a tendency for some students to see English as a 'soft' area of the curriculum, one that does not require any real expertise but

simply the ability to put pen to paper. When teaching grammar as a discrete subject, explain to your students that English has its own technique, just as science or maths do. In order to meet the technical demands of the subject, they must learn about the complex nature of language – how to use it accurately so that they are freed up to develop the more imaginative side of their work.

As well as discussing technique with your children try to find, on occasion, some more original ways of studying grammar. It is all too tempting to use those worksheet exercises that simply ask the children to repeat a particular grammatical technique a number of times. However, although these are useful for reinforcing learning that has taken place, they do not, in my experience, lead to genuine and lasting understanding. Here, then, are some more unusual ways of approaching the direct teaching of grammar. You might like to try these when first introducing a particular grammatical topic, then back them up with worksheets once you are certain that the children really do understand.

- *Make it active*: Children (and indeed adults) enjoy learning that asks them to make an active contribution, rather than simply being expected to sit and write. In addition, learning that has dynamic elements to it tends to stay with us longer, to make more of an impact in our minds. Some children find understanding a topic via a verbal explanation very difficult, and this can be particularly so with the complex language of grammar. For instance, if I were to say 'today we will be studying comparative and superlative adjectives and adverbs, and the addition of the comparative and superlative suffixes "er" and "est"', you would probably switch off immediately. However, a teacher who asks for three volunteers to perform 'big', 'bigger' and 'biggest' will make an immediate (and lasting) impact. He or she might look at the difference in meaning between the three words. The exercise could then be repeated with 'fast', looking at the different between adjectives and adverbs, and so on.
- *Make it a group event*: In the same way that 'active' learning sticks with us, so too does learning in which we take part as a member of a larger group. So, when teaching clause or sentence structure you might name each child in the class

'subject', 'verb' or 'object'. You could then put together sentences by asking the children to come to the front of the classroom and call out a word or words, working together to create the whole. So, the 'subject' child might say 'The girl', the 'verb' child could add 'bought', and the 'object' child might finish the sentence with 'a toy'. By repeating the exercise a number of times, with each student taking an active part in the process, the class would learn about the names of different parts of a simple sentence, and the order in which they come.

- *Make it concrete*: The use of real objects can be very powerful in the classroom, a point I make in Chapter 5 (p. 95). As well as being useful for imaginative work, 'props' can also be helpful in making grammar more real or concrete for your students. For instance, when exploring nouns, collective nouns, and singular/plural verbs, you might ask your children to each bring in a toy. You could then explore the difference between 'The toys are in the classroom' and 'A group of toys is in the classroom', and so on.

An active approach to grammar

An 'active' approach is about letting your students have fun with the language that they and other writers use. By exploring the effects that different parts of the English language create, children begin to experiment with their writing, and learn that working and reworking their own and others' writing can be interesting and enjoyable. In this way, the rules of grammar become internalized, by constant exploration and experimentation. In addition, use of grammatical terminology becomes a natural part of the process of working with language. Here are some ideas for an 'active' approach to grammar. Although these exercises only cover a few areas of the huge subject of English grammar, they should give you some ideas for new approaches to the teaching of the subject as a whole. If you need some information on different grammatical terms, you can find some useful websites in Appendix 2.

Working with other writers' texts

Below are some examples of ways in which your students might interact with the texts that they read and explore the effects that other writers create by their use of words and grammatical constructions.

- *Playing with adjectives*: Ask your students to identify all the adjectives in a piece of text (this could be done with a highlighter). Discuss the effect that these adjectives have on the mood of the piece, for instance creating a scary atmosphere in a ghost-story. Now explore the effect that changing these adjectives would have. Can they find 'better' words? What happens if all the adjectives are removed? Is it possible to describe something *more* effectively without using adjectives? What happens if they put in some 'boring' adjectives, such as 'nice', instead?
- *Avoiding adverbs:* You will find warnings in books on creative writing about adverbs being the sign of a 'lazy' writer. The use of an adverb to describe a verb lets the writer get away without being specific about the action or the person doing it. Consequently this diminishes the picture that the reader might create in his or her mind. For instance, the phrase 'he walked slowly and fearfully up to the door' gives us an idea of how the character is moving, but is not particularly interesting or descriptive. Instead, the writer could say 'he crept up to the door, terrified that the floorboards might creak and give him away'. Again, ask your students to highlight any adverbs in the text they are working with, and to come up with ways of rephrasing the text to replace them.
- *Exploring antonyms*: Go through a piece of text identifying all the adjectives, such as 'cold', 'big', 'happy' and so on. Now ask your students to find antonyms (words that have the opposite meaning) for these adjectives. Encourage them to find several antonyms for each one. For instance, the opposite to 'big' or 'huge' might be 'small', but it could also be 'tiny', 'minute', 'miniscule', and so on.
- *Exploring sentence length*: For this exercise, find a passage that has a high level of tension. Tension is often developed by the use of short sentences, which might indicate a character's

fear, or which could make the reader feel 'jumpy'. Explore the length of each sentence, looking for a series of short sentences that help heighten the tension. Which types of words are in these sentences? What is the shortest possible sentence available to a writer and what must it include (i.e. a single clause with subject, verb, object)? Now look at what would happen if these sentences were joined together with conjunctives, or if subordinate clauses were added. What would the effect be on the overall tension levels of the piece?

Working with their own writing
- *Prefix/suffix competition*: For this exercise, give your children a prefix or suffix, for example 'un' or 'ful'. Now set them a 'competition' in which they must find the maximum amount of words that can be made using this prefix/suffix in a set amount of time. These words could then be utilized in a piece of writing, or in a series of sentences.
- *Justify the choice of words*: When a student shows you a 'finished' piece of writing, ask her to explain her choice of vocabulary and grammar. Highlight any language that seems lazy or sloppy, or that is grammatically incorrect. Ask the child to identify the type of word (i.e. adjective, adverb, noun, pronoun) and suggest that she finds a better alternative. Alternatively, explore with her why the words or phrases she has used are grammatically incorrect, and what must be done to change them. This technique allows you to focus on each individual's grammatical difficulties. It also saves you the wasted time involved in teaching an area of grammar to the whole class that may already have been internalized by most of your children.
- *Brainstorm 'strong' verbs*: Having a bank of really strong verbs can be very useful, especially in creative writing. You could use a brainstorming session with your students, in which they find a long list of these words. (When I say a 'strong' verb, I mean one that indicates a forceful or energetic action.) Start this exercise by giving a sentence with a fairly weak verb, such as 'He threw the football at his friend.' Then look at all the alternative verbs that might be used, and

the effects that these create. For instance, the verbs 'hurled', 'slammed' and 'thrust' would all offer a stronger, more active replacement.

- *Changing tenses*: After your students have finished a piece of writing, ask them to change the tense throughout their work (or to swap their writing with another child and change the tense of his or her work). For instance, they might write a story in the present tense, then change it to the past tense. As an extension of this activity, you could explore the effects of this process on viewpoint, tone and on the reader.
- *Ban 'sloppy' adjectives*: For a week or so, why not ban the more commonly used adjectives? (My vote would be to exclude 'nice', 'good' and 'very'.)

Some thoughts on paragraphing

In my experience, some students have a 'blind spot' when it comes to paragraphing. They produce reams of writing, but without a single paragraph in sight. Why does this problem occur, and what can we do to solve it?

The skill of paragraphing is essentially about learning to structure your writing: understanding the overall 'shape' of a piece of writing and the different ideas contained within it. Here are a few ideas about how you might develop the skill of paragraphing.

- *Write paragraph by paragraph*: When you are approaching a whole-class piece of writing, why not ask your students to write one paragraph at a time? You could set a sentence limit for each paragraph, and ask the class to stop when they have completed the set amount of sentences, perhaps four or five. They could then read out their paragraphs to the class, and discuss whether this would be an appropriate point for a new paragraph.
- *Identify the paragraph's point*: A single paragraph often deals with a single point, using a series of connected or related ideas. Ask your students to identify the points they are making within each paragraph of their writing, and where these points change from one set of ideas to the next.
- *Use the 'four-step' technique*: This technique for essay-writing

is explained in detail in Chapter 4 (p. 73). By using this approach, your students will create a series of paragraphs, each dealing with a single point or idea.

Handwriting

Handwriting is learned early, and any bad habits in the way that we form our letters, or hold a pen, will tend to stay with us long term. Here are a few ideas for working on handwriting with primary-aged children. (You may also find some of these ideas useful for correcting poor handwriting skills in older children.)

- *Use a pen-holder*: Pen- or pencil-holders help small children to learn good posture for holding their pens. These take the form of a small rubber 'sleeve' that is slipped onto the pen. Alternatively, some children may find that moulding plasticine around their pen or pencil will help them to hold it properly.
- *Consider the writing tools*: Using a (poor-quality) ballpoint pen can cause difficulties with handwriting, especially for young children, as they may have to press very hard to form the letters. Look carefully at the writing tools your children are using, and consider whether they may find it easier to write with a felt-tip, especially when they are first mastering the skill of handwriting.
- *Teach correct letter formation*: Most primary teachers will use demonstrations or worksheets that teach their children the correct direction and order in which to form their letters. I have found these worksheets helpful for older children who have picked up bad habits when forming their letters.
- *Use active approaches*: Carrying on from the idea above, you might work with a whole class of primary children, drawing huge letters in the air to encourage correct letter formation. Alternatively, you could take a class into the playground and get them to write enormous letters in chalk on the playground floor, ensuring that they form the letters correctly. As we have seen, this active approach to writing can be very engaging.
- *Use ICT*: For those children who find handwriting very

difficult, why not give them a break at times by allowing them to write on the computer? This will enable them to concentrate on the content of their work, rather than on its presentation.

- *Teach calligraphy*: Make handwriting fun and a source of pride! By learning about the beauty of calligraphy, children can be encouraged to take pride in their writing and to see handwriting as an art form.
- *Explore other forms of writing*: If you have a parent who can write in Arabic, or a teacher in your school who can form Chinese characters, why not ask him or her to come into your class and help you explore different forms of writing and handwriting? Alternatively, you could study Egyptian hieroglyphics with your children.
- *Keep an eye on their technique*: Do keep an eye out for poor handwriting technique. If you are a secondary teacher, don't assume that all your students will have learned or maintained a 'proper' technique. Children who are left-handed may find handwriting particularly difficult, as they will be covering the letters that they form as they write. Watch out for any specific difficulties they might be experiencing.
- *Explore graphology*: You will find some ideas for working on graphology below. These activities are a novel way of motivating your students to look at handwriting, and can be used with a wide age range of children.

Graphology

The graphology exercises below give you just one example of a way to motivate your students in their writing, and to look at what our handwriting 'says' about us. Remember, when we want to motivate children to learn, it is often the more unusual or imaginative teaching strategies that have the most success.

Using graphology will help you motivate your students to analyse their own writing and that of others. It will also encourage them to consider the importance of presentation in writing and show them how our handwriting is as individual as we are. The subject itself is very complex, with many small indicators of personality, and the notes below offer only the briefest of guidelines for you to use in the classroom. (I make no claims to being an expert!)

There is some scepticism about the links between handwriting and personality. However, on a general level, graphology can offer some interesting insights. It is also an unusual way of working on handwriting with your classes.

- *Slope*: A forwards slope suggests someone who pushes themselves towards people, while a backwards slope indicates a person who likes to keep people away. Upright writing, without a slope in either direction, tells you that the person is not really influenced by others but has confidence in himself.
- *Flow*: Just as the way in which we move our bodies indicates our inner state of mind, so the way that handwriting flows can say a lot about a person. When the pen leaves the paper frequently, this shows caution and self-control. On the other hand, writing that flows smoothly shows a decisive, perhaps impulsive, nature. Words in which each letter is printed individually show someone with a keen visual awareness, and may indicate an artistic nature.
- *Pressure*: Heavy pressure on the page suggests a forceful personality, while light pressure shows more sensitivity. Tell your students to feel the back of the paper to check for the amount of pressure they are using. (They may be surprised to discover how hard they are pressing on the paper!)
- *Upper case*: This term indicates strokes which rise above the main body of the writing, such as the top of the letters t, l and h. A highly developed upper case shows somebody with a strongly idealistic, perhaps spiritual nature. People who do not create these developed upper-case letters tend to be more practical.
- *Lower case*: This term means the strokes that fall below the main body of the letters, such at the bottom part of y and g. These understrokes are connected with physical energy, the more pronounced the stroke, the more likely the writer is to be athletic.

Graphology: Activity 1

In my experience, students really enjoy this exercise, and particularly the challenge of working out whose writing they are analysing.

- Introduce your class to the art of graphology, using the notes given above. You could photocopy some notes and hand them out, or write them up on the board.

- Ask your children to write a short piece of text on a loose piece of paper. You could read the text to them, or you could ask them to write briefly on a subject of their choice. Warn them not to include anything that might help identify them! When they have finished writing, ask them to put a mark on the paper to help with identification later on. This could be a number or a symbol, known only to them.

- Collect in the pieces of paper, shuffle them, and ask a student to hand them back out. (Anyone who receives their own text, or a piece of writing that they think they recognize, should hand it back to you so that you can swap it again.)

- Now give your students a set time in which to perform their analysis, using the graphology notes you discussed earlier in the lesson. They could make notes on their analysis in their exercise books, but ask them not to write anything on the sample itself. (That way, you can use it with another class, should you wish.) At the end of the time, they should try to guess whose sample they have been analysing.

- A good way to bring everyone's ideas together is to ask the students to stand up and give a brief analysis of the sample, and the person they believe wrote it.

Graphology: Activity 2

This exercise teaches your students to recognize the importance of clear handwriting. I have found it to be an excellent motivational activity which grabs the attention of a class because it offers them the chance to 'analyse' their teachers. The preparation involved is worthwhile, as the exercise works very well with any year group, and can be repeated with all of your classes if you are a secondary teacher.

- Collect samples of handwriting from teachers and other people who work in your school by asking them to write out a short piece of text. Use the same text for each sample. Try to include some 'surprises', such as the head teacher, the caretaker or one of your catering staff.
- Number the samples and make a note of whose writing corresponds to each number.
- In class, write a list on the board of the people whose handwriting the class are going to 'analyse'.
- Hand out the samples: your students could work in small groups on each piece of writing, swapping their sample with another group once they have finished.
- Compare the results, discussing your students' reasoning and rewarding those who have identified the 'correct' writer.

Working with words

The following ideas give you some interesting and engaging ways of working with words. I have used all these activities with my own classes, and they have proved successful in motivating my students.

- *Hunt the word*: This is an excellent exercise for familiarizing students with using a dictionary. Introduce the activity as a 'game' or a 'contest', to help motivate your class. 'Hunt the word' can be done by individual students, students working in pairs, or by small groups, depending on the ability levels of those in your class (and also on the number of dictionaries at your disposal). The teacher calls out a word, and the class must then race to find the word in the dictionary. As soon as they have found the word, they raise their hands and identify the page reference. You could extend this exercise by asking them to read out the definition, and identify the type of word (e.g. noun, verb, adverb, adjective, etc.). You could also 'reward' the winner by asking them to choose the next word to be hunted. This game could be used with vocabulary from many different areas of the curriculum.

- *Invent the word*: You could begin this activity by looking at the poem 'Jabberwocky', which uses invented words, but ones that still make a kind of sense. For this exercise, ask your students to invent some words of their own. To help inspire them, you could suggest that they are aliens visiting the planet Earth, and that they have to invent words to describe the new things that they see and experience, such as cars, television, houses, and so on. Their words should have some sort of connection with the things that they describe.

- *Invent the language*: In a similar vein to the idea above, this exercise is good for a speaking and listening or drama session. The students work in pairs, using the following scenario. Student A is a visitor to a foreign country and does not speak a word of the language. Student B is a local who does not speak a word of English, only a foreign kind of 'gobbledegook'. Student A must ask for directions in English, for instance to the bank. Student B will then answer in their invented language. After trying the scene, the students should swap roles. Volunteers could then perform their scene to the class. This exercise can result in some hilarious improvisations, and also effectively demonstrates the different ways in which we try to communicate. After watching the performances you could start a discussion on how we use body language and gesture to try to overcome difficulties in communication.

- '*Call my Bluff*': This exercise is shamelessly borrowed from the television programme, and I have found it to be very popular. It is an excellent activity for looking at possible meanings of words via their roots, and would work with younger as well as older students. Divide your class into groups, and hand out one word and definition to each group (use a dictionary to find some unusual words). The group must then come up with one definition for each person in the group. Taking it in turns, the groups then read out their definitions to the class, and the other groups must try to guess or work out the correct definition.

- *Word of the week*: For this exercise, choose one word per week for your class to look at in detail. To give a visual stimulus, you could get your children to make a huge poster of the word to go on the wall. Activities for the 'word of the week' might include the study of closely related words, exploration of the roots of the word, analysis of the category into which this word falls (e.g. verb, noun, etc.), and so on.

3 Writing techniques

This chapter offers an introduction to the 'basic' writing techniques. I have included ideas about how you might introduce, teach and develop these writing techniques at both primary and secondary levels. Not every piece of writing will involve all of the techniques described below, but for extended or 'finished' written work these steps will prove important in achieving the best possible result. In fact, even the simplest piece of writing would benefit from a brief exploration of audience, viewpoint, and so on.

Writing processes

Over the page is a list of the main processes involved in approaching a piece of writing, and a series of questions that your students could ask themselves for each of the steps. You might like to give this list to your classes to use when approaching a piece of writing. The techniques are organized in chronological order, in the way that they might be used when approaching a piece of writing. Some of the questions may be subject to the choice of the teacher, for instance the form of the writing and the audience it is aimed at. The list assumes that a 'starting-point' or inspiration for the writing has already been set.

Preparing

Select a form	*What's the best format to say this in?*
Know your audience	*Who is my writing aimed at?*
Think about your viewpoint	*Where do I stand in relation to my reader?*
Think about your style	*What kind of language should I use?*
Think about timing	*What tense and other time features do I use?*
Brainstorm your ideas	*What ideas do I already have?*
Research facts/ information	*What else do I need to know?*
Map your ideas/points	*How do these things connect?*
Select your material	*What do I need? What don't I need?*
Plan your writing	*How should I structure the piece?*

Writing

Draft	
Review	*What's good or bad about it and why?*
Edit	*How can I improve my piece of writing?*
Redraft	
Check for errors (proofread)	*What technical mistakes have I made?*
Consider presentation	*What's the best way to present this?*
Final draft	
Review the finished product	*Is this as good as it could be?*
Evaluate the finished product	*How can I make it better next time?*

Notice that three of the steps (Draft, Redraft and Final draft) have no questions to answer, and this is because the writing is actually taking place. Your students may be surprised at how much else there is to do when creating a piece of writing. Some of the steps may be taken quickly, by making a decision. Others, such as redrafting, will take longer. If you can get your students into the habit of working through these processes, they will hopefully come to follow them automatically.

The following sections provide a more detailed explanation of each of these processes, and some imaginative, unusual ways of approaching them. I have included a variety of ideas that might help you find new ways of writing across the curriculum and age range.

Selecting a form

In many instances the selection of a form in which to write will be a decision made by the teacher. Finding an imaginative form for a piece of writing can be crucial to engaging your children's interest. There is no reason why these imaginative, unusual forms should not be used in all areas of the curriculum, as you will see from the ideas below. Here are some unusual ideas for using these forms, which cover a wide range of curriculum areas and age groups, in class.

- *Story-writing* (Infant Science) 'Teddy's Big Adventure'. Teddy accidentally gets left behind by his owner, and he must then find his way home. In Teddy's way is a river, which he must work out how to cross. He tries various different materials to see whether they sink or float, so that he can make his raft. Children could research the story by exploring different materials, to see which would be suitable for making Teddy's raft. They could follow this research by writing the story.
- *Film-script* (Secondary Geography): Students write the script for a short film about an environmental disaster, such as the *Exxon Valdez* oil spill. They could incorporate extracts from television news reports of the time, or about current environmental issues. They could also research the subject by writing to organizations such as Greenpeace. As with any play- or film-script, the chance to act out or video the work at the end of the process will increase your students' motivation and engagement.
- *Interviews* (Junior History): A study of the Civil Rights Movement in the United States, and specifically the life of Martin Luther King and his assassination. Students work as police officers, studying the historical data, interviewing witnesses to the crime, writing up witness statements and

police reports, and so on. This work could lead to an exploration of the racist attitudes of some people at the time.

- *Newspaper article* (Junior RE): A report on the death of Jesus during a study of early Christianity, as seen in the newspaper *The Jerusalem Echo*. The report could include descriptions of the crucifixion from Roman soldiers, interviews with the followers of Jesus, quotations taken from the Bible, etc.
- *Recipes* (Secondary Science): A chemistry experiment, written up in the form of a recipe. To make the process more interesting, the students could 'mimic' the language and style of a popular chef, such as Jamie Oliver or Delia Smith. They could then use a video camera to create a TV show in which the chef explains the recipe and demonstrates the experiment. This would help increase your students' engagement with the writing.
- *Instruction booklet* (Junior PE): After learning a new game, such as rounders or netball, the children write an instruction booklet about the rules and directions for playing the game. To make this activity more engaging, you could ask them to choose an unusual 'audience' for their writing, such as an alien with three arms, telling them to alter the rules to fit this unusual player!
- *Packaging* (Infant Art/Design): The children invent a new chocolate bar, cereal, toy, etc., and must then design and create the packaging that goes with it, including suitable wording. As an extension, they could create posters or television adverts to promote their new product.

Knowing your audience

The audience at which our writing is aimed plays a crucial role in determining the language we use, the style in which we write, the type of presentation we use, and so on. In my experience, having a 'real' audience for their writing can be one way of truly engaging our students in the writing process. Here are just a few ideas about how you might find a 'real' audience.

- *Writing for others in your school*: Ask your students to write a book aimed at young children, but give them a specific audience to work for. In a mixed infant and junior school, you could do this by inviting a group of infant children into your junior class. You could then ask your children to research their specific needs and wants before preparing books for them. Your students could read their finished books to or with the infants, and obtain feedback from the children about how well the books worked. Alternatively, your class could create books for a school library, or for other teachers to read to their children.

- *Writing for the internet*: There are many websites that now publish children's stories or poems, and this is an excellent way of motivating your students to produce high-quality work and rewarding them for the writing they produce. You can find a list of some sites that publish children's work in Appendix 2.
- *Writing to a penpal*: Again, having a real person with whom to exchange letters or emails can be a stimulating experience. Your penpals could be children from other countries (see Appendix 2 for details of some websites that support this activity). Alternatively, your penpals could be students in other schools in this country, or perhaps Year 7 students in the local secondary school. This is an excellent exercise to help with preparing Year 6 children for what to expect when they move to secondary school.
- *Writing to an author*: Why not get your class to write to an author they particularly admire? Many authors will respond to the letters or emails that they receive from their readers, and this can be a very inspiring experience for young writers/readers. (See Appendix 2 for details of some author websites.)

Thinking about viewpoint

Viewpoint can be quite a difficult concept for young writers to understand, but it basically means where the writer stands in relation to their reader. For instance, in a first-person narrative, the writer talks through the perspective of 'I', telling the reader about their own thoughts and feelings (or those of the first-person character they are playing). Encourage your students to experiment with different viewpoints: how does this piece of writing work with a first- or third-person narrative? Again, an unusual or imaginative approach works well when dealing with viewpoint, and can also help encourage the skill of empathy. Here are just a few ideas for thinking about and working with a first-person viewpoint.

- *The toy's story*: With younger children, you might ask them to bring in a favourite toy, and then tell the story about the day that the toy came to school, but from the perspective of the toy and using a first-person narrative. You might start this activity by bringing in a toy of your own, and telling the children your own toy's story, using a 'toy-like' voice. You could extend this idea by asking your children to take their toy on a trip around the school or the playground, viewing the world through the eyes of a small toy, and making notes about how the toy would see these strange things from its perspective.
- *Diary writing*: Older students could be asked to write the diary of a famous person or historical character, again from a first-person perspective. Although this idea works well for an English lesson (for instance the diary of a character in a set text), it could also be applicable to other areas of the curriculum, such as History or Religious Studies. This exercise is particularly good for developing the skill of empathy with another person.
- *The object's view*: A slightly more bizarre approach would be to use a 'character' that is actually an object. For instance, the viewpoint of the football that was used during the FA Cup Final. How did the football feel about all those fans chanting? How did it feel about being kicked so hard, and ending up in the back of the net?

Thinking about style

There are a variety of different aspects that go to make up the style of a piece of writing. The decision about style will depend a great deal on the form of the writing and the audience it is aimed at. As we have seen previously with grammar activities, an active approach to the study of writing always works well. Here is an activity on style that could be used at a variety of ages within the classroom.

Ask your students to study various extracts of writing, for example a children's storybook, a 'literary' novel, a newspaper report, a history textbook, a recipe, and so on. Then ask them to examine the style that the writer uses in these extracts, referring to the pointers below. When they have done this, discuss the effect of these different aspects of style. Here are some of the things that you could ask your students to consider.

- *Audience*: What type of audience is this writing aimed at? How old is the projected audience? How can we tell this? Is the piece successful in appealing to this audience?
- *Language*: What type of vocabulary does the writer use? Are they long or short words, or a mixture of both? Will the audience understand the words that are used, or is the writer trying to sound 'clever'?
- *Grammar*: Is Standard English used, and is the writing grammatically correct? Or, is a more formal, talkative style apparent? How does this use of grammar relate to the form and audience of the piece?
- *Formal or informal*: Is the audience being addressed with formal or informal language? How can you tell this? Why has a formal or informal style been chosen?
- *Interest level*: Is the writing interesting or gripping for the reader? What is it about the style of the piece that creates this interest level?
- *Genre*: Is the piece of writing in a particular genre, that requires a certain type of mood? For instance, a horror story would require a very different style and mood to a romance. (See Chapter 5 for some more thoughts about genre.)
- *Tone*: Does the writer 'sound' as though they are in a particular mood? Is the style of the piece 'happy' or 'sad'? Is the writer trying to evoke a specific emotion in his or her audience?

After working on the extracts in this way, you could follow up the activity by asking your children to rewrite the piece, but in a completely different style, which aims at a totally different audience and consequently is written in a very different way.

For instance, a 'dry' piece of writing from a history textbook could be written in the style of a football match report. Similarly, when working on a piece of writing of their own, ask your students to experiment with a variety of different styles, perhaps writing a paragraph in each style and then reading them to a partner for his or her opinion.

Thinking about timing

As well as thinking about where they stand in relation to their audience, your students also need to work out a 'time setting' for their writing. One of the most important features of timing is clearly the ability to write in (and stick to) the correct tense. As well as considering which tense to use, you should also encourage your children to play with other aspects of timing, particularly when writing a creative piece. I have included some ideas about how they might do this below.

Although there are formalized and 'correct' uses of tense in different forms of writing, it is important for your students to understand the reasons why this is so, if they are to internalize the process. As with their audience, writers need to think about where they stand in relation to the piece of writing. Are they describing something that happened in the past, something that is happening in the present, or something that will happen in the future? Here are some ideas about the logic behind choosing a tense.

- *The story*: The majority of stories are written in the past tense. To help your children understand why this is, talk about the imaginative process of inventing a story. The best stories are created first in our heads, rather than being made up as we write. Encourage your children (however young they are) to run a 'film' of the story in their imagination, 'watching' the characters and the events that take place. Then, the process of writing the story becomes simply a case of describing the events that have just taken place, in (of course) the past tense.
- *The essay*: When we are writing an essay, unless we are describing historical events that have taken place in the past,

we are giving an interpretation of a text or situation, or making a series of statements that we believe to be true, and these are being made by us at the moment we write the essay. Consequently, the present tense is the logical tense to use.

- *Instructions*: If we were writing a list of instructions to build a piece of furniture, we would be describing the series of actions that somebody would need to take in their 'present'. Consequently, we would use the present tense, for instance 'First, nail the wooden board into the base ...' If the instructions were details of a forthcoming school trip, the future tense may well be used, for instance 'next week we will be going to ...'

One of the problems that can arise with the use of tenses is that children may slip between the past and present tense. Here are some thoughts about how you might address this problem.

- *Shared reading*: Ask your children to read out a finished piece of writing to a partner, or to a small group. The audience can help point out where changes of tense occur.
- *Spot the mistake*: As an extension of the idea above, you might also like to present your class with a piece of writing in which there are several deliberate changes in tense. For instance, you could jump from the past to the future tense and then back again. The children could raise their hands every time they hear a 'time jump'.
- *Past, present, future*: This activity provides a simple but fun and active way of working on these three tenses, and on conjugating verbs. It is particularly suitable for infant and junior children, but could also work with Year 7 or 8 students. You will need a fairly open space to work in. Divide your class up into groups of three, with one of the three students being 'past', one 'present' and one 'future'. Now the group must choose a verb, for instance, 'swimming'. The three students then demonstrate an action that involves this verb, and the rest of the class must guess the verb they are acting, giving their answer in the correct tense. So, for the verb 'to swim' you would have the answers 'he

swam'; 'she swims/is swimming'; 'she is going to swim/will be swimming'.

In addition to considerations about the correct tense, encourage your students to think carefully about the timing and pace of each piece of writing. Here are some areas that you might like to work on.

- *Balancing description and action*: The pace of a piece of writing depends a great deal on the balance of these two features. For instance, if a story is heavily descriptive this will slow the pace right down for the reader. However, a story that is pure action, without even an adjective to slow the reader down, will generally be fast-paced and gripping. The two examples below demonstrate the differences in pace that can result within descriptive or action-based writing. You might like to use this as a writing activity, asking your students to write a close, descriptive study, and then a fast, pure action story. This exercise will also help to develop your students' knowledge about language terminology (for instance, you might ban the use of adverbs and adjectives from the 'pure action' piece of writing).
- *Slow-motion moments*: Many films make use of slow motion at a particularly pivotal point in the story. Encourage your students to consider which moments in their writing might deserve the 'slo-mo' treatment and why. They could then experiment with expanding one of these moments into a piece of 'slo-mo'. This might be done by extending a short piece of descriptive writing, or by describing a piece of action in great detail.
- *Sentence length*: The length of the sentences in a piece of writing will have a surprisingly strong impact on its pace. As you will see in the example below, long sentences tend to slow down the pace of the writing, allowing the reader to 'sit back' as they picture the story. On the other hand, short sentences add pace and movement to writing, and can help develop an edgy, tense feeling.

Example 1: Descriptive (slow pace)
Jane stood in front of the doorway, collecting her thoughts, delaying her decision until the last possible moment. As she waited for her courage to arrive, like a slow train moving into the last station on the line, she studied the door in front of her. It was crafted from an ancient-looking wood, the handle a simple metal ring. Jane glanced down as she stretched her arm out towards the handle. Her hand was shaking, and the deep red nail polish on her nails reminded her of blood. She retracted her hand and took two deep breaths, brushing her fringe from her face with her pale fingers. She stood a while, contemplating everything that might happen once she went inside. Then, at last, she was ready. She summoned up every ounce of courage in her body and grabbed the handle. Turning it slowly, and pushing the heavy door open in front of her, she stepped into the hallway.

Example 2: Action (fast pace)
Jane ran to the door. She grasped the handle and turned it. Pushing the door open, she moved inside. She sped down the hallway and reached the room at the far end. No one there. She turned and ran in the opposite direction.

Brainstorming

The brainstorm (also known as the spidergram or scattergram) has become ubiquitous in schools, and with very good reason. The brainstorm provides an excellent way of gathering ideas together, and is particularly useful for a whole-class introductory session when first approaching a new topic. There is also the chance to impose an initial structure on our thoughts and ideas, and to develop lateral thinking by the use of arrows which create a series of sections and subsections. Our students are encouraged to use brainstorming in many different areas of the curriculum, but we do perhaps need to think of ways of making the technique more effective and interesting for them. Here are some ideas about how you might do this.

- *Use colours*: This idea ties in with mind-mapping (see p. 57 for an explanation of this technique). Using colours helps us to segregate our ideas into different areas, and also makes the brainstorm more visually appealing. For instance, when creating a brainstorm on 'Our World' as a geography topic, you might use blue chalk or pens for water-related ideas, green for ideas connected to plants, brown for the land, and so on.

- *Make the brainstorm big!*: In my experience, big (or preferably huge) words and images are particularly appealing to children. Why not take your class into the hall, or another open space, and create an enormous brainstorm on your topic? The most important words or ideas could be written in the biggest text, with those coming off them slightly smaller, radiating out from the centre of the brainstorm. This technique will also help your children identify which ideas are more important than others.

- *Make the brainstorm active*: Similarly, an active approach to brainstorming could be very appealing. For instance, you might divide your class into groups and take them into the playground. Then each group could be given some chalk and asked to brainstorm on the playground floor, preferably as big as possible. You could even use this idea for a whole-class playground brainstorm, putting the topic idea in the centre of the space, and then giving each group an area of the topic/playground to work on.

- *Use images*: The very word 'brainstorm' brings a striking picture to mind. Why not create a worksheet for individual brainstorms with a picture of an exploding brain at its centre? You could talk with your students about how the brainstorm is literally an explosion of the contents of their brain on to paper. (This gruesome idea is likely to appeal to them!)

- *Use a tight focus*: As well as gathering ideas on a topic together, brainstorms can also be used with a tighter focus. For instance, you might brainstorm all the vocabulary connected to a single word (such as 'cat') in order to write some poetry.

Researching

Once they have established what they already know, your students will need to decide what other information or facts are required before they can work on their piece of writing. This could be as simple as reading some children's story books to explore the type of language that is used, before writing a children's book of their own. It could be a matter of identifying some quotations to use in an essay on *Macbeth*, and looking up details of some different productions of the play. Or it could be as complex as researching an entirely new topic for a history project in considerable depth. Below are some possible sources for your children's research.

- *Texts*: I have deliberately used the word 'texts' rather than 'books' here, because some of the most useful and accessible textual information will be found in magazines and newspapers. Before approaching research using texts, you might like to do some work with your children on ways of finding information within a text, for instance looking at indexes and how they are laid out. You may also need to look at how to scan and take notes (see Chapter 6 for some thoughts on these areas).
- *ICT*: Teachers can now draw on a range of ICT resources, and for research the most useful of these will be CD-ROMs and the internet. If your library or IT department does have a bank of CD-ROMs, do check with them whether any of these might be suitable for your research. The internet is also a hugely useful tool for research, although it is surprisingly hard to use it effectively without consuming vast amounts of time. There is so much material out there that it is easy to find yourself moving laterally from the original point of your research, although this is not necessarily a bad thing. (See p. 56 for some thoughts on keeping the research focused.) A good search engine is crucial: I particularly like Google for its simplicity and the relevance of its search results.

- *People*: Some of the most valuable and interesting research can be done by interviewing 'experts' on a particular topic. For instance, to research a piece of writing about their family history, your children might interview their grandparents, aunts, uncles, etc. Similarly, one of your children might have a parent who is an expert in a particular field. Invite them in to talk about their subject for your research, whether it is cookery, gardening, astronomy or feng shui! Alternatively, you might ask your children to write letters or emails to someone who is an expert on the relevant topic.
- *Trips*: For many children, a class trip is one of the most exciting and interesting events of the school year, and the chance to get out of the classroom for a few hours, or even for a whole day, is very appealing. However, a trip also offers a chance to find fresh perspectives on a topic you are studying, and may inspire some excellent writing.

When researching, and particularly when using the internet, it is very tempting to go off at a tangent when you find some facts or information that interest you. It could be that you have plenty of time and are happy for the research to proceed in this way. However, teachers are often faced with the need to get through written tasks (and the curriculum) as quickly as possible in order to fit everything in. How then can you help your students to research efficiently and use your class time most effectively?

- *Identify what information is needed*: Ask your students to create a list of questions that they need or want answered. Their research should then focus on answering these questions. They could even set themselves a specific number of questions to aim to answer in a single lesson.
- *Provide focused research material*: If you are going to be researching in the library, you could liaise with the librarian before the lesson to find the texts that are most likely to be useful to the children. These could then be presented on a 'research table' for the children to look through. Alternatively, if you were researching a topic on the internet, you might give your students a list of the best or most useful websites.

- *Keep them 'on task'*: Going off task can be a problem, especially when using the internet, with all its temptations, and also if you have a class with challenging behaviour. In order to keep your children 'on task', set them targets for their research. For instance, after fifteen minutes you might stop the class and ask one or two students to talk about what they have discovered. Alternatively, you could give each child a worksheet that must be completed, identifying what they found out during the lesson and where they found it. This could prove a useful way of collating whole-class information on a single topic.
- *Set research as a homework task*: The beauty of this approach, particularly with a large project, is that your children will naturally differentiate their learning. The more able or enthusiastic child will seize the opportunity to delve deeply into a subject that they enjoy. For the less able or less well motivated, try to ensure that the topic being researched is something that really captures their interest, or provide them with a well-targeted set of homework questions.

Mind-mapping

The mind-map is the brainstorm's big brother, and if you haven't already used this technique then do give it a try. While the brainstorm gives us an effective way of noting initial ideas or information, the mind-map offers a wonderful method of organizing these points before we start to write. It is particularly good for giving a structure to complex ideas, those that are too difficult or diverse to keep in your head at one time. It also allows you to include information that has only a lateral connection to the main topic, and to explore different tangents and connections within a subject, that might not be immediately apparent at first glance. The mind-map works in much the same way that our brains work: we store huge amounts of information in our brains by making connections between different facts, ideas, and so on.

As with the brainstorm, the use of colours can help you to create an effective mind-map, especially if these colours are linked to the topic and sub-topics being studied. Mind-maps can be used across the range of curriculum subjects, and for a huge variety of different topics. They can be used to give a structured overview of data or information that you already have, or they might be used to brainstorm initial thoughts on a particular topic. For instance, you might map the characters in a novel, including relevant quotations from the text, relationships between the different characters, and so on; you could map the natural world to show the links between different geographical features; you might map the progress of different battles during World War II. Perhaps the best way to understand the mind-map is to look at an example. The mind-map pictured in Figure 3.1 is based on the question: 'What role does technology play in your life?' The points given in the mind-map show the way that a typical student might answer this question.

Selecting material

Deciding what to include, and what to leave out, can be a real challenge when we are writing. This can prove especially problematic when our students are working under exam conditions. They are so keen to include everything they know that they fail to answer the question and may also run out of time. Thus the selection of suitable material is a vital skill to learn and practise. In essence, selecting the appropriate material depends a great deal on the purpose of the writing. Is its main purpose to answer a specific exam question, to study a topic in detail, to entertain, to inform? Here are some ideas to help you when teaching your children to select material.

- *Identify the purpose of the writing*: Take the time to discuss this with your children: talk about why they are writing on this particular topic, and what their audience will expect. Is the writing a brief summary, or an in-depth study? Are they trying to entertain or inform their audience? What does the reader most need or want to know? Is the purpose simply to answer the exam question in a way that gains as many marks as possible? If this is the case, what will the examiner want to see included?
- *Answer the question*: To succeed in their exams (in whatever subject), your students will need to answer exam questions

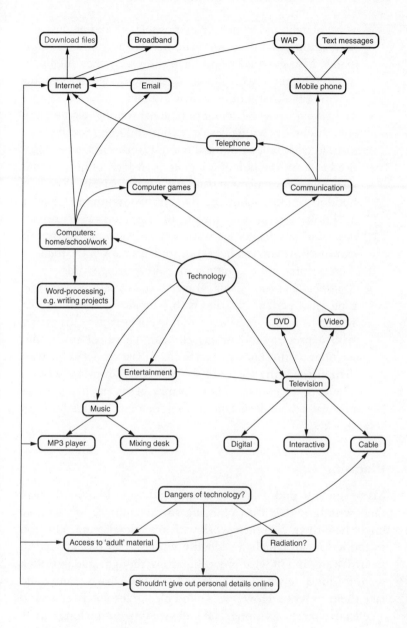

Figure 3.1 Mind-map: '*What role does technology play in your life?*'

as accurately and concisely as possible, including just the right amount of information and material to gain maximum marks. You can find plenty of tips on how they might do this in Chapter 4, which looks at essay-writing, and Chapter 7, which looks at writing and assessment.

- *Make it interesting*: In a piece of fictional writing, where there is no 'right' or 'wrong' answer, your children must learn to include what will be of most interest to the audience. They need to learn the skill of gripping the reader, of how to find interesting vocabulary and invent exciting events. You can find lots of ideas about effective creative writing in Chapter 5. Look also at the stream of consciousness exercise described in Chapter 1 ('warm-up exercises', p. 12) which explains how you can help your students narrow the focus of their writing and choose the most interesting words.

- *Something unusual*: Given 30 pieces of writing on the same topic, it is perhaps the one with a touch of originality that will stick in the examiner's mind. For instance, the writer who expresses him- or herself with a dash of style, who includes a little-known (but relevant) fact or detail, or who demonstrates the ability to think laterally around a subject. There is, of course, a fine balance between including an unusual, telling detail and the irrelevant fact included only to shock.

Planning

Many students find it hard to understand why they should plan their writing, rather than plunging straight into it. In class, we might help them plan their work with a whole-class introduction to the lesson, in which we identify what should be included in their writing, and in what order. In exams, though, students often seem fearful of 'giving up' the amount of time that a plan would take them to write. However, a good plan is absolutely crucial to an effective piece of writing, and will save time in the long run. A well-thought-out plan will assist in structuring a piece of writing, as well as helping the student to stay on track when answering a question. (It also helps to stave off panic if the student's mind suddenly goes blank halfway through an answer.)

When planning for a piece of writing, I would advise using a series of brainstorms, one for each paragraph or part of the work. Not only does this method encourage your students to structure and paragraph their writing correctly, but it is also a time-efficient method of planning. In addition, this format allows the overall planning of the writing as a whole, after which the student can go back and add in additional ideas, quotations, facts to include, and so on. You can see an example of brainstorms being used for planning in the next chapter (see the section 'Planning an essay', p. 69).

From first to final draft

The pressure on teachers to cover the curriculum can lead to a situation where we get our students to 'bang out' pieces of writing one after the other, with only minimal thought given to drafting, reviewing, editing and redrafting the work. When time is short, the temptation is to have at least one quantifiable piece of writing to 'prove' that we have dealt with each area of our subject or subjects. In addition, we have surely all experienced the student who brings us a piece of rough writing and claims to have 'finished' the work. However, many of the skills inherent in effective writing are learned from the processes that take place in-between the first and final drafts. To emphasize the point, here is a list of just some of the skills that are utilized when developing a draft into a final piece of writing.

- *Content*: Identifying irrelevant content, repetition or 'waffle' and removing it; ensuring that all important or relevant ideas or facts are included; checking the accuracy of facts or statements.
- *Structure*: Ordering ideas in the most logical and fluent way; using paragraphs correctly and appropriately; checking the overall 'shape' of the piece; finding a good opening and ending.
- *Vocabulary*: Avoiding ambiguous words; ensuring correct meaning and context; choosing the best or most interesting vocabulary; cutting out unnecessary or boring words; ensuring that the level of difficulty matches the reader's ability and expectations.

- *Spelling*: Checking the spelling of unfamiliar words; identifying spelling errors and correcting them.
- *Grammar*: Correcting grammatical errors; altering word order or sentence structure to make the piece 'read better'.
- *Punctuation*: Correcting errors of punctuation; altering sentence structure and punctuation to avoid excessive sentence length; adding appropriate punctuation to indicate tone of voice.
- *Tone*: Correcting slips from formal to informal language; maintaining a constant tone throughout; avoiding patronizing the reader.
- *Style*: Appealing to the identified audience; using the appropriate style of writing for the chosen form; developing an interesting, gripping and individual style.

How, then, can we both encourage and develop the ability to draft and redraft, with the steps of reviewing and editing in between? Here are some ideas that you may find useful.

- *Quick draft*: Encourage your children to see their first attempt as a 'quick draft'. You could set a specific length of time for this, depending on the type of work being done. For this draft, you might allow them to concentrate on the content, rather than worrying overly about the sentence structure, grammar and accuracy of spelling.
- *Test draft*: Similarly, I have used answers written under timed conditions during a test to provide a first draft (for instance for a piece of coursework). When writing under test conditions, even the less well-motivated students do tend to produce a reasonable amount of work, which can then be redrafted to produce a higher-quality piece of writing.
- *Draft on the computer*: When I write my books, I use a computer from start to finish. My 'first draft' might simply be a list of chapter titles, with further subheadings added in a 'second draft'. The third and fourth drafts might consist of writing under each subheading. At this stage I may feel that the material needs a complete reordering, and so I might eliminate some chapters or combine them with others. Because all this drafting is done on a computer it takes only a

matter of moments to do this cutting and pasting work. So I would advise you to encourage your students to do as much of their drafting as possible on computer, whether at home or in class. The word processor is a wonderful tool – why not make use of it? In addition, of course, the computer can give us some help with proofreading our writing: highlighting incorrect spellings and identifying poor grammar. (See Chapter 10 'Writing and ICT' for more ideas on the use of computers when writing.) Having said all this, though, the fact that they must give handwritten answers in their exams means that we must still ask our students to practise writing longhand.

- *Read it back*: When a student brings you a 'finished' piece of work, ask them to read it back, either to you or to a partner. This process will help them see the importance of redrafting to correct errors and to make the writing sound better.
- *You be teacher*: Children love being given responsibility, so why not get them to swap their first drafts over and 'be teacher'? You could ask them to mark, comment on or correct their partner's work. The edited first drafts can then be returned to their owners for further correction and rewriting.
- *Set a focus*: For weaker writers, it can be disheartening to redraft their work, because there are so many mistakes to correct. For these students, set a specific focus for the redraft. This could be looking up any spellings about which they are uncertain; it could be taking great care with punctuation and ensuring that every sentence has a full stop; or it could be dividing their work up into paragraphs.

Presenting the final draft

So, when that final draft is at last ready to be presented as a finished piece of work, what can be done to display it in the best possible way? Here are some thoughts on the presentation of writing.

- *Suit the presentation to the writing*: The way in which the final piece of writing will be presented depends a great deal on the type of writing that your children have done. An essay might be either neatly handwritten or carefully typed up, while a more imaginative piece of writing might use a more original style of presentation.

- *Use imaginative presentation techniques*: With many pieces of writing, the form of their final presentation can be both imaginative and attractive. For an 'ancient' historical document, you might use the old favourites of staining the paper with tea or coffee, and then burning or tearing the edges slightly. For a children's book, you might offer your students the chance to create a book cover using the computer, and so on.
- *'Publish' the work*: As we have already noted, having a 'real' audience for their writing is an excellent way of motivating children. Why not 'publish' your class's final drafts, either as a class book of writing or perhaps via the internet?

Reviewing and evaluating

Finally, your children's writing will really benefit from time spent reviewing and evaluating it. This might take place as a whole-class activity, in which the students share their work and review or evaluate each other's writing, or it could be an individual activity, in which students complete a worksheet asking them questions about the finished work. Asking our children to take this step, rather than viewing it as a part of marking, will save time for the teacher. More importantly, it encourages our students to look back at a completed piece of writing and consider the content, structure, use of language, punctuation, and so on. By analysing their own work in this way, we can help them learn to set targets for the development of their writing.

The review and evaluation could focus on one particular area, for instance how technically accurate the work is, or how interesting and relevant the content. Alternatively, and perhaps more effectively, you could ask your students to look back at all the steps listed at the start of this chapter, and consider which areas they still need to develop, and which they have been successful in.

Part 2

Writing across the Curriculum

4 Essay-writing

For some of us, essay-writing comes naturally. We see the logic in following one point with another, of using relevant evidence or quotations and of crafting our sentences together to create a coherent chain of thought. However, for many of our students, essay-writing retains a mystique, a sense that there must be some 'magic' involved. This is, of course, nonsense. As we have already seen, the skills and techniques used in writing *can* be learned, and this chapter gives you a number of ideas about how you might make essay-writing as straightforward and interesting as possible. It also gives a detailed explanation of the four-step essay-writing technique, a strategy that I have developed, and which has proved successful for me, especially with my weaker students. In addition, you will find ideas for developing essay-writing, as well as examples of how things go wrong, and what might be done to fix them.

Perhaps the most important part of teaching essay-writing is to go through lots and lots of essay questions with your classes. Show them the techniques involved by articulating the process of writing an essay as you work through it with them. Share as many exam questions as you can with your classes. There is no need for them to write out a full essay every time they look at a practice question: they could simply write out a series of plans to show how they would answer the question in full in an exam. Although many of the points in this chapter will be of interest primarily to secondary school teachers, there are also plenty of ideas and strategies here that could be introduced to younger students on a simpler level.

Some basic tips

The following tips deal with the overall process of essay-writing, and some of the areas where mistakes are most likely to occur.

Many of the points I make below cover areas in which I have seen my own students make errors. These tips will need to be reiterated over and again: essay-writing is a complex business and it takes time to get it right.

- *Answer the question*: It is absolutely vital that your students learn to do this. An essay that does not answer the question might as well not have been written at all, for all the marks it is going to get. So, right from the start, drum this point into your students. Some ideas about how to teach your children to answer the question are given below.
- *Use the correct tense*: In most cases essays should be written in the present tense, as though describing something (for instance, an event in a novel) that is happening in the current moment. One obvious exception to this is when recounting or discussing factual events from the past.
- *Avoid mixing tenses*: Unless it is intentional, tell your students to stick to one tense throughout their essays. The exception to this might come in a history essay, in which events from the past are recounted, and then comment is given on the impact of these events in the present day.
- *Avoid slang*: Essays should be written in Standard English, and slang should not be used, unless in direct quotation from a text.
- *Avoid abbreviations*: Similarly, it is a good idea to avoid abbreviations such as 'I'd' or 'it's', simply because they make the essay style sound a little too informal.
- *Use a simple (but formal) style*: Encourage your students to use clear and simple language and expression. Although the style should be formal, there is no need for them to try to sound 'posh', as this is unnecessary and will usually backfire.
- *Don't be afraid of a personal reaction*: There will often be scope within exam questions for some type of personal comment. This might be indicated by a question that says 'Comment on your own feelings about/opinion of this … '.
- *Give an interpretation of the evidence*: I always advise my students to suggest, rather than to insist upon the points they make. This allows scope for them to introduce unusual ideas, or to make comments about which there is some

disagreement or controversy. For instance, they might start a point by saying: 'It is possible that …', or 'One interpretation of this is …'. You can find some more ways of starting a sentence to suggest a point or interpretation at the end of this chapter (see 'Interpretive starters').

- *Take care with the 'royal we'*: Unless it is used with care, the 'royal we' can make the style of an essay seem rather pompous or self-satisfied, especially with younger students. There is also the danger that 'we' statements can seem overly confident, rather than interpretative (a problem if the statements are incorrect!). It is fairly simple to minimize the use of 'we'. For instance, instead of writing 'We can see that …', your students might say 'It could be argued that …'.

Planning an essay

When planning an essay, I would advise the use of a series of brainstorms, as described in Chapter 3 ('Planning'). Each brainstorm should cover the contents of one paragraph, with perhaps four or five different points that are going to be included, and any relevant quotations or facts that the student is planning to discuss. You can see an example of this planning method in Figure 4.1. I have based the essay plan on the very generalized question used in Chapter 3 (Figure 3.1), 'What role does technology play in your life?' Figure 4.1 shows the brainstorm plan that might be made in answer to this question by a typical student. Using brainstorms in this way to plan an essay has a number of advantages.

- *Time efficiency*: In an examination essay, this method offers a quick way of giving overall structure to the piece. As I have mentioned, students tend to view time spent planning as 'wasted time', especially under exam conditions. However, with practice, your students will find that using a time-efficient method for planning will actually allow them to write their essay more quickly and effectively.
- *Sticking to the point*: Having a single 'main idea' at the centre of each brainstorm will help your students stick to the point they are making in each paragraph.

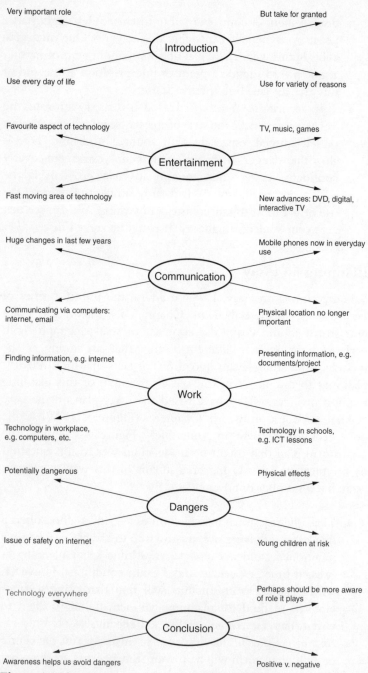

Figure 4.1 Planning brainstorms: *'What role does technology play in your life?'*

- *Creating a structure*: Each brainstorm should provide enough material for a single paragraph. Not only will this approach help your students remember to paragraph their essay, it will also allow them to 'play around with' the structure of their writing. Before they start writing, they can check that the ideas follow a logical progression, and if they do not, they can swap some of the brainstorms around.

- *Introduction and conclusion*: It is often hard to decide exactly what you are going to say in an introduction or conclusion before the essay has actually been written. By leaving a brainstorm at the start and end of their plan, the students can work out the overall structure and focus of their essay, then complete the plan by deciding what the best introduction and conclusion would be.

- *Adding in ideas*: In an examination essay, creating a series of brainstorms for a plan allows some flexibility when the student does come up with new ideas during the course of writing the essay. These ideas can be slotted into the overall structure by adding them to the brainstorms.

- *Demonstrating ideas*: If a student runs out of time when writing an examination essay, the examiner may take their planning into account when they mark. The brainstorm plan will give a clear indication of what the student was planning to write, had he or she not run out of time.

Answering the question

As I have already mentioned, you should stress over and over to your students that they *must* answer the question that they have been asked. In an exam they will only gain marks for answering the question, and it is vital that they learn how to do this. Here are some strategies for 'answering the question' that you could share with your classes. (You will find some more ideas about approaching exams and exam questions in Chapter 7.)

- *Read the questions first*: In an exam where the students are given a text of some type to comment on, the very first thing they should do is to read the questions they will be required to answer on that text. This should be done *before* they read the passage, as well as after. This will help them because they will have the questions already in their minds while they are reading.

- *Use the question to answer the question*: As well as helping your students stick to the question, this technique is also useful for those who have trouble getting started in exams. I have found it particularly helpful for Year 9 students answering their SATs exam papers. Tell your students simply to use the question as a statement with which to start their answer. For example, if the question asks them 'In the passage, what three things does Fred hate about his school?', they could start their answer 'In the passage, Fred hates three things about his school. The first thing that he hates is . . .'

- *Write out the question*: The physical action of writing out the question at the top of the page is a very strong reminder of the question they are meant to be answering. In addition, having the question there in front of them will hopefully remind them to stick to it as they write their essay.

- *Make a plan*: I make no apologies for repeating this point, because a well-thought-out plan will not only help your students structure their essays, it will also help them stick to the question. The plan is made with the question fresh in the mind, and it also helps keep the student 'on track'.

- *Keep referring back*: It is all too easy to become sidetracked when writing a long essay. Encourage your students to re-read the essay question (which is, of course, written at the top of their exam paper) frequently during their exams. Each time they re-read the question, they should make a mental check that they are still sticking to answering the question. If they are not, they should complete that sentence or paragraph quickly and then get back to the point.

How to quote

Finding and using quotations does seem to cause problems for students, whether from a novel, a poem, a factual source, and so on. The skill of quoting is something that we need to teach our students. Here are some ideas and tips for you to share with your classes.

- *Use short quotes*: When quoting, students often assume that they need to use a whole sentence or even a large chunk of text. Remind the student that the examiner will have access to the text that they are discussing. Consequently, they only need to include enough of a quotation to make their point, or to show which part of the text they are making reference to. A short quote of about five to fifteen words is usually adequate.

- *Find the important bit*: Teach your students to hunt out the most important part of a phrase or sentence for their quote. For instance, one of the lines from Christina Rossetti's poem 'A Birthday' is 'My heart is like a singing bird'. If a student were discussing this simile, they might say 'Rossetti uses the simile "like a singing bird"', rather than quoting the whole line. As mentioned above, when referring to a text (especially one that is reproduced in the exam paper), it is usually safe to assume that the examiner is able to read it too.

- *Have a bank of quotes*: When writing on a text, or on a particular topic area, encourage your students to find a bank of quotes that could be used in exams and coursework essays. These quotes should cover a range of issues (for instance themes, characters, imagery in a novel) and should be easily accessed (for instance written in the front of their text, if this is allowed).

- *Don't say 'I quote'*: The use of this phrase can jar in an essay, and could well lose marks for your students. Encourage them instead to say 'The author says ...' or 'The character says ...', and so on.

The 'four-step' essay-writing technique

As both an English teacher and a writer, it occurred to me that it must be possible to offer a technique for writing essays: one that would enable the less skilled to succeed in what can be a difficult writing task. The technique described below is one that I have developed over the years while teaching my students to write. By breaking down some of my own essays into their constituent parts, I was able to identify the subconscious strategies I had used to construct these extended pieces of writing.

The magic of this technique lies in its simplicity. If the student is willing to follow one step with the next in a logical way, then he or she will succeed in writing an essay. This technique has worked for me with weak, poorly motivated students, as well as with borderline C/D GCSE candidates, and also with those working at A/A★ standard. It has proved useful when introducing essay-writing for the first time with students in Key Stage Three. In fact, there is no reason at all why it should not also work on a more basic level with junior school children, as an early introduction to essay-writing techniques. The technique involves four steps, each of which provides the student with one or two sentences. Put together, these sentences will then create a single paragraph of the essay. The steps are repeated until the essay is finished. I developed this technique for writing English essays, but it is equally applicable to essays in other areas of the curriculum, such as History, Geography or Science.

The quality of the finished essay will obviously depend on the student's grasp of the ideas or facts that they are writing about, and on their ability to express themselves. However, the four-step technique helps avoid that familiar problem whereby students start off dealing with the essay question but then go off at a tangent. It also gives the less able a chance to write a reasonable essay of their own.

The four steps are as follows:

1. *Statement*: State something that is true, or make a comment on the subject.
2. *Evidence*: Give evidence or factual detail to support your initial statement.
3. *Explain*: Explain how the evidence links to your initial statement.
4. *Develop*: Develop your ideas, elaborating more fully, or finding a further link.

For weaker students, the fourth step can be left out, and the resulting essay will usually still be good enough to gain a reasonable grade in an exam or a piece of coursework. Here are two examples of the four-step technique in action. To show that this technique is applicable across the curriculum, my examples relate to English Literature and Science (specifically Biology). The first example looks at imagery in Shakespeare's play *Romeo and Juliet*; the second example explores vertebrates and their evolutionary sequence.

Example 1

1. *Statement*: In *Romeo and Juliet*, Shakespeare makes much use of imagery connected to light.
2. *Evidence*: While Romeo waits below Juliet's balcony, he tells us 'The brightness of her cheek would shame those stars, / As daylight doth a lamp.'
3. *Explain*: Here Romeo uses his words to paint a picture that is saturated with images of light. Just as the daylight is brighter than a lamp, so Romeo feels that Juliet's beauty is so radiant, it would 'shame' even the stars.
4. *Develop*: These images of light contrast strongly with images of darkness, and of the night, particularly at the end of the play, when the lovers die together in a dark tomb.

Here is the full paragraph, as it might appear in an essay:

In *Romeo and Juliet*, Shakespeare makes much use of imagery connected to light. While Romeo waits below Juliet's balcony, he tells us 'The brightness of her cheek would shame those stars, / As daylight doth a lamp.' Here Romeo uses his words to paint a picture that is saturated with images of light. Just as the daylight is brighter than a lamp, so Romeo feels that Juliet's beauty is so radiant, it would 'shame' even the stars. These images of light contrast strongly with images of darkness, and of the night, particularly at the end of the play, when the lovers die together in a dark tomb.

Example 2

1. *Statement*: Animals with a backbone (vertebrates) are divided into five classes, and these classes of vertebrate are linked by evolution.

2. *Evidence*: The five classes, in order of evolution, are fish, amphibians, reptiles, birds and mammals.
3. *Explain*: The first vertebrates were fish, and from these came the amphibians. The amphibians gave rise to reptiles which eventually evolved into both birds and mammals.
4. *Develop*: These five classes of vertebrates are divided into cold-blooded creatures (fish, amphibians and reptiles) and warm-blooded animals (birds and mammals).

Again, here is the full paragraph, as it would appear in an essay on this subject:

Animals with a backbone (vertebrates) are divided into five classes, and these classes of vertebrate are linked by evolution. The five classes, in order of evolution, are fish, amphibians, reptiles, birds and mammals. The first vertebrates were fish, and from these came the amphibians. The amphibians gave rise to reptiles, which eventually evolved into both birds and mammals. These five classes of vertebrates are divided into cold-blooded creatures (fish, amphibians and reptiles) and warm-blooded animals (birds and mammals).

Now let's consider each step in more detail.

Writing the statement
Depending on the curriculum area, and the subject of the essay, the statement might be something that is 'true' (i.e. an accepted fact), or a comment about something that you believe to be 'true' (i.e. an interpretation). Encourage your students to couch any 'facts' that they are unsure about as a possibility, supposition or interpretation, 'suggesting' that something might be true, rather than stating it as an absolute fact. In the example above about vertebrates, I have stated the information as a fact, because it is accepted to be so within the scientific community. However, there are actually various different options for writing this statement (or any statement), especially if a student is unsure

about whether what they are saying is interpretation or fact. Here are some examples:

Suggestion 'Scientists generally divide animals with a backbone (vertebrates) into five classes, and have found evidence that these vertebrates are linked by evolution.'

'Scientists generally divide' suggests that it is scientists, rather than the writer, who make this division; 'have found evidence' explains that there is evidence for this supposition, again found by scientists.

Mixture of suggestion and fact 'Scientists divide animals with a backbone (vertebrates) into five classes, and these classes of vertebrate are linked by evolution.'

'Scientists divide' again suggests that it is scientists, and not the student writing, who divide animals into these classes; 'are linked by evolution' gives a statement of fact.

Finding the evidence
The evidence to support the statement may take various different forms. It is worth taking the time to help your students experiment with using each of these forms.

- *Factual detail*: Some subjects and topics offer students 'factual details' to use. These facts stretch across the curriculum and, as we have seen above, include generally accepted terminology, as well as 'true facts' such as a person's date of birth or when one country invaded another, and so on.
- *Quotation*: Quotes may take the form of a line, phrase or sentence from a text that illustrates the statement. They might also be a quote from a textbook in which the author makes a statement that supports the initial contention.
- *Events*: Instead of using quotation, your students might describe an event in support of their statement. For instance, in an English essay they might use something that happens in the story to illustrate a character's personality. Alternatively, in a history essay, the event described could be an actual historical incident related to the original statement.

Explaining the link

The third step involves exploring the link between the initial statement and the evidence that has been given. The ability to make these links between comment, and evidence for that comment, is one of the most important skills in essay-writing. Exploring or explaining the link forces the student to ensure that the initial statement has been well thought-out, and that the evidence given does actually support the statement that has been made.

Exploring the link might be a simple explanation of how the quote or evidence given does actually support the statement that has been made. For instance, in the *Romeo and Juliet* example above, the writer notes that the picture Romeo paints with his words is 'saturated with light'. Explaining the link can also involve a development of the statement and the evidence. For instance, in this example the writer goes on to explain exactly how the light-based image itself actually works.

Developing the point

The fourth step – development – is perhaps the hardest for students to grasp. However, as I have noted, the first three steps will still provide them with a reasonable essay. The fourth step is perhaps the difference between a student who might achieve a grade D–F at GCSE, and a student who is capable of achieving a grade A–C. Development of a point might take place in one of the following ways, or in another way that the student feels is relevant.

- *Further explanation*: Development might involve a further indication of ways in which the evidence supports the initial comment.
- *Links to other areas within the topic or text*: It might also be about finding a link to another area of the subject being explored. For instance, when writing about a fictional text, students might explain how their point relates to other events or significant factors within the text.
- *A connection to the social or historical context*: The development could be the student making a connection to the wider context of the subject being discussed. To give an example,

when writing about the theme of the supernatural in *Macbeth*, a student might develop the point by discussing the historical context in which the play was written, and the attitudes to witchcraft at this time.

- *A lateral connection*: The development could also be the student making a lateral connection to another idea or area within the topic. For instance, a student writing about an author's characterization might link the characters in a text to those in the author's life.
- *A wider issue*: Similarly, the development could involve suggesting or explaining a link to a wider issue within the topic. For instance, a student writing about the environment within a science essay might link the points made to the current global environmental situation.

Introductions and conclusions

Writing introductions and conclusions is perhaps one of the hardest aspects of essay-writing. In my experience, many students find it hard to start an essay, and end up writing an introduction that has little real connection to the topic under discussion, or one that simply states irrelevant facts, as seen in the examples below (see the section 'When essay-writing goes wrong'). Part of the problem is that the introduction to an extended piece of writing is often best done *after* the body of the writing has been finished. This is fine in a coursework essay, which can be drafted and redrafted, perhaps on a computer, but it is impossible to do in an examination situation. What advice then can we offer our students about writing introductions and conclusions?

- *Give a taste of what is to come*: The best introductions give a 'flavour' of the essay as a whole, an overall 'taster' of the points that will be made, but in a very general way. The best writers will find a way to hint at what is to come, both in the things that they say and also in the language that they use.
- *Use the question to start the essay*: As I pointed out in 'Answering the question' earlier in this chapter, a good way to start an introduction is to turn the question that has been asked into your opening statement. (This technique is

especially helpful for your weaker students, and for those who have difficulty getting their essays underway.) For example, if the question asks 'What factors led to the start of the Second World War?' the student might begin the essay by saying 'There were a number of factors which led to the outbreak of the Second World War.' As well as helping them get started, this will also keep them on track with answering the question.

- *Use the introduction to introduce the subject*: This point might seem obvious, but it is often ignored. The 'taste' mentioned above is basically an introduction to the writer's viewpoint on the question that they have been asked.

- *Find a lateral point to make*: In the example given below of an essay introduction, the point made about the language of movement is actually quite peripheral to the essay's content as a whole. However, it provides an interesting and engaging way into the subject for the writer and the reader.

- *Use the conclusion to summarize the content*: The conclusion should provide an overall, general summary of what has been discussed in the essay. Encourage your students to try to come to some sort of conclusion, especially if the essay question has asked for specific comment on a topic. For instance, in answer to a question asking 'Which of these two characters do you most sympathize with?' the student should include a summary of the opinions they have given in the conclusion and come to a definitive answer.

- *Don't be afraid of the personal*: In the example below, you will see that the essay ends with a highly personal note. Giving an individual view or comment on a subject can be a strong way of concluding an essay, especially one that is about a subject of importance to the writer.

- *Don't be afraid of the emotional*: Similarly, if it is relevant to the subject under discussion (for instance in an interpretive piece of writing, or one that analyses a fictional text), a strong conclusion will often involve the declaration of an emotional response to the subject.

- *Avoid direct reference to the content*: When unsure of what to write, it is tempting to make the introduction a list of what will be in the essay. The student starts by saying 'In this essay

I will be looking at x, y and z and saying how . . .' This will generally not gain them any marks, and is also not really a valid introduction.

Perhaps the best way to illustrate the points above is to look at an example of an introduction and a conclusion. The following example demonstrates how an introduction and conclusion to one specific essay could be written.

Essay question: Discuss the role that dance should play within schools, considering its strengths and weaknesses as part of an increasingly crowded curriculum. What problems must be solved if dance is to play a full and valuable role in the educational experience?

Introduction

People use the language of movement when an experience touches them deeply – we might say 'I am walking on air' or 'my heart leapt' – and these instinctive metaphors give us an insight into the fundamental role that movement plays in our lives. It is understandable that the role of dance and movement within schools has been neglected by teachers: burdened with a heavy workload and a lack of experience in this area, there are other issues that perhaps seem more pressing. However, I feel it is vital to challenge the attitude that sport alone is adequate to satisfy our children's physical needs. There are a huge range of educational possibilities inherent within move-ment lessons – dance helps us to develop not only our physical skills but also our imaginative and creative abilities.

Conclusion

Dance has been a part of my life for twenty years. The expression and insight that it has given me have been instrumental in the development of my character. Dance allows us to express ourselves imaginatively and creatively. It also provides a wonderful opportunity for physical

> activity. If teachers can provide opportunities for their
> children to experience the richness inherent in movement
> and dance activities, I believe they will find its value and
> importance priceless in their students' education.

Interpretive starters

As I have said throughout this chapter, if there is any uncertainty
about a 'fact', then students should be encouraged to use sentences
which only suggest the points made, rather than state them. For
instance, this might be helpful if your students are unsure about
whether a point they are going to make is entirely correct, or if the
essay is interpretive rather than factual. Here is a list of
'interpretive starters': ways that your students could start a
sentence to *suggest* that what they say is true, rather than stating
it as a definite fact.

- It could be claimed that ...
- Some commentators believe that ...
- One possible interpretation of this is ...
- It is possible to view this as ...
- One way of viewing this is ...
- It could be argued that ...

Essay-writing with the most able

When working with very able students, essay-writing provides
an excellent chance for us to stretch our students' writing skills
to the limit. Extended writing, in the form of essay work, lets the
most able develop their writing in a wide range of ways. They
might explore different ways of structuring their work, or look at
using linguistic techniques to give their writing more interest.
Here are some strategies for working on essay-writing with the
most able.

- *Develop the use of tone*: The best essays use a writing style that
  reflects the tone of their subject, and you should encourage
  your students to develop this skill. To give an example, if a

student is writing about a piece of text with a sad, emotional theme, this could be reflected in the choice of words and style of the essay.

- *Develop the use of language devices*: A good essay-writer might use language devices within the essay, whatever the subject. For instance, the writer might use repetition to link together a series of ideas, repeating a word or image several times throughout the essay. He or she could use a metaphor to deepen an explanation or alliteration to make the essay sound more appealing. The technique of 'listing in threes', in which the writer (or speaker) lists three points in order, building in power and emphasis as they do so, could be used.

- *Develop the use of pace*: Pacing a piece of writing is a subtle skill. The most able of your students should find it possible to work with the length of their sentences, and their words, to vary the pace of the writing within an essay. With practice, a sense of flow and movement can be achieved.

- *Develop 'a voice'*: Similarly, the best essays give the reader a sense of the 'voice' of their writer. A satirical essayist might use a cynical tone, while a more emotional essay-writer might use a passionate voice to make their points. A consistent 'voice' which is maintained throughout the essay will make the writing far more appealing to the reader.

- *Give the reader something to chew on*: An essay that includes a surprise fact or comment, or that concludes by leaving a question hanging in the air, can be very powerful. The most polished essay-writers amongst your students should be encouraged to make their essays striking for the reader. For an examiner marking a pile of essays all on the same subject, the writer who stands out from the rest, or who says something original, will catch their attention (and perhaps be awarded a few vital extra marks).

When essay-writing goes wrong

Below you will find examples of the two most common mistakes that students make when writing essays. The illustrations I give are taken from 'real-life' difficulties I have encountered when teaching my own classes. For each example I give a commentary on the mistakes that have been made, and suggest some ways of solving the problems.

Example 1: Irrelevant facts
Essay question: Discuss the characters of Macbeth and Lady Macbeth, exploring the relationship between them, and the way that this relationship changes during the course of the play.

Shakespeare was born in 1564 in Stratford-upon-Avon. He lived there before moving to London to work as an actor and writer. His play *Macbeth* is about a man called Macbeth who kills the king. The king's name is King Duncan. After he has killed King Duncan, Macbeth himself becomes king. Macbeth's wife is called Lady Macbeth ...

Commentary: In this example, the student starts his/her essay with a list of facts, none of which has any relevance to the question that has been asked. Counter this problem by revisiting the skills required to answer essay questions. Work through the ideas given in the section on 'Answering the question' earlier in this chapter.

Example 2: Listing
Essay question: Analyse the imagery used in the poem 'Upon Westminster Bridge' by William Wordsworth.

In 'Upon Westminster Bridge' Wordsworth uses lots of imagery. He uses lots of personification and similes. He personifies the city, saying that it 'wears' the beauty of the morning. He personifies the river, saying it 'glideth at his own sweet will'. He uses the simile 'like a garment' ...

Commentary: The problem here is that the student 'lists' the images that he or she has found, but does not explain any of them, or offer any further development of the points. In the four-step process described in this chapter, the student is taking only the first two steps. To overcome this problem, show your students how to explain the evidence they give, and how to develop the points that they make in further detail.

5 Creative writing

Creative writing encompasses a range of forms and can take place across the school curriculum. Although story-writing, scripts and poetry may traditionally be seen as forms that are used within the English lesson, they also provide a useful way into writing in many different subjects. Creative writing appeals strongly to children – they welcome the chance to use their imagination, to invent new people or imagine new storylines. In addition, the children that we teach are surrounded by creative writing in their everyday lives through the whole range of the media. So, although some of the ideas in this chapter will be more applicable to English lessons in a primary setting, or to the English teacher in a secondary school, I also give plenty of ideas about using creative writing in other areas of the curriculum.

Creating a fiction

As teachers, we spend much of our time creating 'fictions' for our students, whether this is conscious or not. For instance, a teacher who uses the 'strict and scary' model described in my book *Getting the Buggers to Behave*[*], is creating a fiction about themselves as a teacher. Few of us are actually 'strict and scary' people in our lives outside school. The teachers who use this model in their professional lives are (I should imagine) unlikely to shout at or be 'scary' with their friends and family. However, they find that by creating this fiction about themselves within the school they get better behaviour from their students.

---

[*] Sue Cowley, *Getting the Buggers to Behave* (London: Continuum, 2001).

Our children, too, are complicit in the fictions we create. In fact, schools are reliant on the students' willingness to go along with these fictions, in order to maintain a sense of order and control. There is no real reason why children should behave for and obey their teachers, but, in the majority of cases, they do. I have been told by parents on several occasions that their children will do something if a teacher tells them to, but will not take the same attitude if it is their parents asking them. This is at least partly due to the 'fiction' of teachers as figures of authority. In my experience, children enjoy being part of a fiction, and as teachers we can utilize this interest to engage with and motivate our students in their writing. This chapter explores how you might use creative approaches and different forms of creative writing across the curriculum, including different ways of creating fictions to develop our children's writing.

The importance of genre

One of the best ways into any piece of writing for the teacher is via genre, and this applies especially to creative writing. The following sections deal with genre, looking at how it can be used across the curriculum and examining its different elements. I also explore how you might create an inspiring atmosphere for genre writing, and how you can take an 'active' approach to this topic, in which the students are encouraged to play with different genres.

Genre is a French word which literally means 'type'. The children of the twenty-first century are positively steeped in genre: through the movies they watch, the books they read, the television programmes they see and the computer games they play. Certain genres can be particularly helpful to the teacher, because they really capture the children's attention, for instance science fiction, crime, horror. The Harry Potter phenomenon has seen an upsurge of interest in magic, and the fascination with this genre has been reinforced by hugely popular television programmes such as *Buffy the Vampire Slayer*. So, by approaching creative writing via genre, we can spark our students' interest and get them motivated in their work.

Genre across the curriculum

Although genre is very useful for approaching story-writing in an English lesson, it can also be used in other areas of the curriculum. Here are just a few ideas about how you might use genre in a cross-curricular way, especially within the primary classroom.

- *Ghosts* (Maths): Creating a board game which takes place within a haunted house (this could be done by the teacher, or by the students). In each room of the house is a ghost or other spooky creature. The players must answer a maths question correctly to win against the ghost and move on to the next room. The final room in the house could contain 'treasure' or a reward of some type. Writing activities could include creating the rules for the game and writing the questions that the ghosts are going to ask.
- *Pirates* (Geography): Drawing and labelling a map of a treasure island (again, either the teacher or the students could do this.) On the map are various geographical obstacles, such as sinking sand, rocks, an impenetrable jungle, a volcano, and so on, which prevent the pirates from reaching the treasure. When designing their maps, the children could research each geographical feature and learn more about it, including how and why it is dangerous. They could also build a three-dimensional model of the treasure island. The writing done in response to this work might include description of the different geographical features, writing pirate diary entries, a set of instructions on how to find the treasure, and so on.
- *Horror* (Design and Technology): The children build a three-dimensional monster of their own. This could be done on a large scale using boxes, kitchen rolls, etc., or on a smaller scale using Lego or Meccano. They could then write a list of instructions about how to build a monster, or they could write a story in which the monster comes to life and goes crazy!
- *Science fiction* (Science–Astronomy): The teacher puts the chairs in the classroom into rows, in the same layout as on an aeroplane. The children are told that they will be going on a journey into outer space, in their very own spaceship. As

they fly away from the Earth, you could introduce the various planets that they travel past. They could be asked to make a 'logbook' for the spaceship, writing down notes about each planet that they pass. Another written response to this might be for them to send letters home to their families, describing the different planets that they have seen. To make this work more exciting, your spaceship could encounter some asteroid belts on the way, which hit the spaceship and throw the children about inside!

The elements of genre

Asking our children to write within a genre also gives us a wonderful chance to exercise their writing skills. They must select the correct elements to include: the right types of character, the likely locations, the appropriate words and terminology. They must also think carefully about audience expectations when writing within a specific genre. Generally speaking, genres follow set rules, although many of the best genre stories either break or subvert these rules in some way. A story in the magic genre is almost honour-bound to feature witches and wizards, while a story in the crime genre is going to feature a criminal, a victim and a detective at the very least. The following list gives an outline of the various elements you could explore within a genre when using it as a basis for written work.

- Characters
- Location
- Storyline
- 'Lighting' and atmosphere
- 'Props' (objects)
- Costume or clothing
- Type of dialogue
- Likely vocabulary
- Plot events or features

When first introducing the subject, a useful exercise is to ask your students to pick one genre, and list the 'standard elements' that they would expect to find. For instance, in a crime story you might have the following features:

- *Characters*: victim, criminal, 'scapegoat', witnesses, detective, police officers.
- *Location*: back alley, police station, bank, get-away car.
- *Storyline*: a crime takes place; the police work to solve it; the criminal is caught.
- *'Lighting' and atmosphere*: dark, foggy streets; tense, scary atmosphere.
- *'Props'*: weapons, handcuffs, evidence, photofit posters.
- *Costume or clothing*: police uniforms, a blood-stained shirt, prison uniforms.
- *Type of dialogue*: formal language used by police; criminal might use slang.
- *Likely vocabulary*: crime, criminal, victim, witness, forensics, fingerprints, etc.
- *Plot events or features*: the discovery of a body, the clue that is a 'red herring'.

Setting an atmosphere for genre writing

The use of genre offers you a wonderful opportunity to create an atmosphere or mood in your classroom. By doing this, you will spark the children's interest, and engage their attention, inspiring them when they come to write. Here are some ideas for setting an atmosphere for genre writing in your classroom.

- *Ghosts*: Blackout the classroom, or work in a space that has blackout facilities, such as a drama studio. If possible, find a tape with spooky whistling-wind-type noises. When the children arrive, hand out torches and ask them to enter the room very quietly, so as not to disturb the resident ghosts. Once inside, they could sit in a circle while you read them a scary story. Alternatively, why not create a whole-class story by going around the circle, with each child adding a word or sentence of their own? This approach to the genre could be used to introduce and inspire the writing of ghost-stories.
- *Crime*: Set up a corner of your classroom where a crime has taken place. Add some props to act as clues, and put a line of 'police tape' to keep the children out. At the start of the lesson, tell your children that they are going to be working as detectives, and that they have to work out how the crime

took place, by examining the evidence, interviewing witnesses, and so on. This work could be used to introduce a new text, such as *Romeo and Juliet*, with the crime scene and clues relating to the evidence from the story. Written work might include police reports, witness statements, newspaper stories, and so on.

- *Historical*: Set up your classroom as a village from a particular historical era (for instance the medieval period). The children could dress as characters from that time, and be given the jobs that people would have done. You might use this work to explore living conditions, and how, for instance, malnutrition and plague could have taken hold as a consequence. Writing from this setting might include diary entries, newspaper reports, 'aged' documents, and so on.

An active approach to genre

As well as supplying you with endless imaginative and inspirational ways into written work, genre can also be useful for the study of language and looking at how writing is structured. A good way of exploring this area is to introduce extracts from various different genres, then to examine the language and style that the writers use. Here are some useful questions to focus your study.

- *Vocabulary*: Which words in the writing are specific to its genre? What type of words or phrases are they (nouns, adjectives, adverbial clauses, etc.)? Is the vocabulary from a different historical period? What would happen if we changed some of the genre words in the piece?
- *Colloquialisms*: Are there any words here that are specific to a region or dialect? Is slang used? How does this relate to the genre?
- *Formal/informal*: Is the language used in a formal or informal way? How does this relate to the genre itself? Which specific words, phrases or grammatical features tell us that it is formal or informal?
- *Pace*: What type of pace does the writing have? Is it fast or slow-moving? How is this effect achieved, and how does it relate to the genre being used? What sort of level of tension is there in the piece?

- *Sentence structure*: How are the sentences structured? Are they long or short, simple or complicated?
- *Overall structure*: How is the piece structured as a whole? What conjunctions or connectives are used? What ideas do we find in each paragraph? How does the piece open and close? How does this relate to the particular genre?
- *Tone*: What tone is the writer creating, and how is he/she doing this? Which words help to convey tone or emotion? How do these relate to the genre?

Playing with genre

After looking at different genre writing in this way, you could develop the work by asking your students to rewrite the extracts, changing them into another genre. Playing around with genre in this way can also prove a very useful and highly motivating approach to texts in general. Students seem to love 'subverting' the original form of a piece of writing. When they do this, they will be learning about and developing an understanding of the conventions of various written forms. In fact, the best writing is often that which does subvert or play with convention in some way.

I experienced a wonderful example of the way that forms and genres can be played with or subverted when I was teaching my very first Year 9 class in preparation for their SATs. We had studied *Romeo and Juliet* in some detail, and we were working on the party scene, where the young lovers meet for the first time. We had also been exploring slang and dialect, discussing the language that Shakespeare used, and how his plays might sound today. I set an activity to translate the party scene into modern-day language, adding slang or using dialect as the class wished. Two of my students, who came from an Afro-Caribbean background, worked together to produce a fantastic patois version of the scene, which we performed in class. Here is an extract from their scene, showing the impressive way in which they were able to play with the original words and subvert the form in a way that I believe Shakespeare himself might have enjoyed.

Rochon and Juju

[*Enter* MASTER CARLTON, MISS CAROL, JUJU, TYRONE, 'ELPER and guests.]

CARLTON: Welcome ladies and gentlemen. Which one of you lovely ladies want fi dance? If you say no a corns you a grow pon dem foot, come bus' out the tune, nam and drink until your belly bus!

[*Ladies kiss their teef and look away.*]

Come rest yourself cos.

CARLOS: Jesus peace a thirty years since mi last see you.

CARLTON: A nuh that long. It was at Lucil wedding.

CARLOS: Oh yes, mi remember that well. That was in the old days when we were young and lively.

CARLTON: Those were the days man!

ROCHON: Who's that pretty woman over deh so?

SERVANT 1: Mi nuh know sir.

ROCHON: She kinda nice you know. We warn fi teck her to mi yard tonight. Mi just go teck a little breeze over deh so.

Here are some thoughts about how you might subvert or play with genre in your classroom. These activities could be used with the very youngest writers, as well as with your older students.

- *Subverting audience expectations*: When we read a story, we do so with certain expectations about what will happen and how the characters will behave within that genre. This is especially so with the genre of fairy-tales: these stories have simple, traditional plots, and use highly stereotyped characters. By subverting audience expectations, writers can create some wonderful and humorous effects. For instance, the author Babette Cole confounds audience expectations by rewriting Cinderella as 'Prince Cinders', and making her characters behave very differently to the originals.
- *Changing the form*: Similarly, changing the form in which a story is presented can produce some interesting and often

hilarious results. For instance, you might rewrite and perform the story of 'The Three Little Pigs' in various different styles:
- as a football match report
- as a TV news story
- as a 'Jerry Springer'-style chat show
- as an opera
- as a soap opera.

- *Updating and changing the language*: In the example above, from *Romeo and Juliet*, the power of the piece comes from the way in which the language has been updated and changed into patois, while still retaining the meaning of the original. Other ideas for updating and changing language might include a Victorian melodrama rewritten in the style of 'Ali G', or conversely a modern-day crime story rewritten in the style of Jane Austen.

- *Changing the perspective*: Certain genres tend to use set perspectives. For instance, the crime story is normally written from the viewpoint of the detective, or the thriller from the perspective of the hero. By shifting the perspective you can achieve some very interesting results. For instance, in the hilarious 'Dr Xargle' books, the writers view Earth and Earthlings from the perspective of visiting aliens.

Finding inspiration

Although the need to find inspiration is not limited to creative writing, it is perhaps the area in which it plays the most important role. Finding inspiration for writing might be about discovering the initial spark for a story, or about choosing ways to develop a piece of descriptive writing more fully. Inspiration comes in many shapes and forms: here are just a few suggestions for how you might find inspiration yourself, and how you can help your students to find inspiration of their own.

- *Starting points*: Giving your children some 'starting points' for their fiction will help inspire them to create a story. You might give them a character, an emotion, a place and an item from which to develop their writing, for instance:

- king / angry / haunted house / spell–book
- dog / lonely / castle / key
- astronaut / terrified / alien planet / spaceship.

- *Props*: Children find having an actual item to work with very engaging, especially if it is something that seems 'out of place' in the classroom. Again, we are taking them outside their 'ordinary' lives and into a fiction where the imagination can roam freely. Working with a prop can lead to ideas for characters, places, events, and so on. There are a huge range of things that can act as 'props', and it is useful to have a box of different props in your classroom to help whenever inspiration is needed. In this box you might have different types of bags and purses, some jewellery boxes, feathers, stones, money from different countries, and so on.

- *Associations*: Inspiration can be found by making associations between one thing and another. For instance, you might bring an exotic piece of fruit into the classroom, and ask the children what sort of places they associate with it. You could start by asking them what the exotic country is like where this fruit is grown. When working on using the senses (see below) you might work on associations between a certain smell or sound and a particular place. You could brainstorm these associations with your children to help them find inspiration for their writing. What smells do they associate with a hospital, or with a shopping centre? What sounds do they associate with a zoo, or with an airport?

- *Bag of words*: When approaching a piece of creative writing, why not have a bag of words that your children can dip into? The words in this bag should be unusual, ones that stimulate the imagination. They might be words that the children do not yet know, but that they could either look up in a dictionary or simply use the sound of the word as an inspiration. You could even have a selection of bags, one for places, one for characters, one for types of weather, and so on.

- *Music*: Listening to a piece of music can inspire your children's imagination and make them think of different moods, places, people, etc. By starting a writing lesson with time spent listening to music, your students should become more focused for their work. This will also give them the chance to move inside their heads and use their imaginations, to allow the fictional world to take hold.

- *Take them into the world of the imagination*: For this exercise, ask your children to close their eyes (they could do this lying on the floor in a comfortable position). Now move them into an imaginary world, by taking them on a 'journey'. Your journey could be to a desert island, into an enchanted forest, into outer space, anywhere really. Give them a brief description of their journey and what they see, but do not be too specific – let their imaginations fill in the details. For instance, in the enchanted forest, ask them to look around. What do they see? Perhaps they visualize a house or a strange creature. Tell them to walk slowly up to whatever they see and look at it in detail.

Using your senses

Generally speaking, we do tend to use some of our senses more than others when we are writing. Most people focus on what they see and hear when writing a story, but of course we also have the chance to explore taste, touch and smell. Here are some ideas about ways to get your children using their senses to inspire and develop their creative writing.

- *Senses worksheet*: This approach is useful for brainstorming vocabulary before writing a poem or story. It can also be used for approaching certain topics in other areas of the curriculum, for instance looking at the impact pollution has on people through their sensory responses to it. Draw up a worksheet on which each of the senses has one column: see, hear, taste, touch and smell. The children then brainstorm around a topic or a word, under the headings of each of their senses.
- *Removing one sense*: For this exercise, you deprive your children of one of their senses, and this encourages them to use their other senses more fully. For instance you might remove the sense of sight, by blindfolding the students in turn. They could then be given a variety of objects to touch,

smell, listen to (and even taste). This could lead to some excellent descriptive writing, but it could also be used to explore different types of material in a science lesson. Alternatively, you could remove the sense of touch, by asking them to put their hands behind their backs. They could then be asked to describe how different objects would feel, but without actually touching them.

- *Colours*: This is an exercise that I did when I was at school (and have remembered ever since, which proves it was highly engaging). You may well be sceptical about it, but do give it a try. If nothing else, it provides an excellent way into writing work about colours, and also creates a strong sense of focus in the classroom. The students are blindfolded, and then a sheet of coloured paper is put in front of them. Ask them to touch the paper and focus very hard on 'feeling' the colour. Although it may be only a matter of luck, when I did this exercise at school there were certain people in my class who could 'feel' the colours correctly most of the time. Alternatively, you could ask the other children in your class to describe the colour being touched to the child who has been blindfolded, giving hints as to what the colour might be. For instance, with the colour blue they might use the words 'water', 'ocean', 'sky', and so on.
- *Weather*: Ask your children to shut their eyes and imagine a particular type of weather (you specify this), for instance a storm. Now ask them to move through their senses, one at a time, as you say them. Start by asking them what they can see, then what they can hear, and so on. Again, this work can lead to some excellent descriptive writing. It also encourages the children to empathize with their characters, and to feel what a character might feel, for instance if they were stuck outside during a storm, or trapped on a desert island in the heat.
- *Place and sound*: For this exercise, the whole class is involved in creating a place by using their senses, specifically their hearing. The best way to do this exercise is to have the whole class lying in a circle on the floor, with their feet facing out of the circle and their heads nearly touching. In this way, they each get the best possible 'sound effects'. The

teacher specifies a place for the children to create through sound, for instance a prison building up to a riot, a ship in a storm, a haunted house on a windy night, a Victorian asylum, and so on. The children should start quietly, adding sounds as and when they feel it is appropriate. The sound effects then build up to a climax, before ending, either by fading out, or by stopping abruptly. Preferably the class should decide as a whole (without any signal) when it is a good point to fade out or stop the soundtrack. When done properly, this exercise can be extremely powerful. You may find at first that your children are too noisy, or that they do not work well together. However, with practice, you will find that the 'places' created can be extraordinarily powerful and inspirational. You might also choose to tape this exercise, either to play back to your children, or alternatively to use as a 'mood' tape for writing inspired by this work.

Writing fiction

Writing stories for the sake of writing stories is a wonderful opportunity for children to use their imagination, a faculty that is perhaps underutilized in schools. Fiction-writing allows us to work in the realm of the imagination, and let our minds run free. It can also give children a valuable outlet for their worries and emotions, offering as it does a pretend world in which they can explore those issues that they find troubling.

Although writing a story just to learn about writing a story is a task for English lessons, there are many other areas where writing fiction can prove extremely useful. As I noted above, story-writing can help children deal with their fears, and for this reason stories might be used to very good effect in a PHSE lesson. The following sections deal with fiction-writing from the perspective of story-writing, although much that is covered is also applicable to writing scripts as well. In addition, this material should prove useful when your students come to analyse the work of other writers.

Creating characters
One of the most exciting things about writing fiction is the chance to create imaginary people, and even creatures, all of our

very own. At first, most writers have a tendency to write about the people that they know, although it could be argued that children have a greater ability to use their imaginations than do adults. The exposure to television and film that is so prevalent nowadays means that, at first, your writers might fall back on copying plots and characters that they have seen on screen. However, by using some of the exercises described above to take your students into their own imaginations, you should be able to overcome this issue. Here are a range of ideas for encouraging your students to create interesting and believable characters of their own.

- *Props*: As I have already noted, children find the use of 'props' exciting and engaging, and these can be used to develop interesting work on characters. For instance, bringing a piece of clothing into the classroom could inspire the children to talk about the different characters who might wear it. Similarly, you might 'find' the bag that belongs to a character (perhaps at the scene of a crime), and look at the contents of the bag to decide the type of person who owns it.
- *What's in a name*: Alternatively, why not give your children one or more unusual names, and ask them to write about the characters that they visualize. Choose a name which has additional layers of meaning or in which the words hint at other, related ones, such as 'Cruella de Ville'.
- *Setting the scene*: Another engaging idea is to set up a 'scene' in your classroom, which the characters have just left. To give just one example I have used myself, put two hands of cards on a table, some coins scattered across the table, and on to the floor, two chairs (one upright, the other overturned), an empty glass and a bottle that has fallen to the floor. Now talk with your children about what has just happened in this scene, and what sort of characters took part in this story. You could even ask some of your students to 'act out' the scene as it took place. This type of work can lead to some really inspired story- or scriptwriting.
- *Hot seating*: This drama technique is excellent for developing characters, and is loved by children of all ages. Ask for a volunteer to sit in the 'hot seat', facing the rest of the class.

This volunteer is going to 'play' a character. This character could be invented beforehand (this technique can in fact be used to 'question' characters that already exist in a text you are studying, whether it is a GCSE text or a children's book). When inventing a new character it is often best to let him or her take shape as you go along, by asking questions that force the person in the 'hot seat' to invent the 'story' of this character on the spot. To give an example of how this might work, the teacher might start by saying 'I understand that you were seen running away from the Royal Oak Public House, covered in blood? Can you tell me what you had to do with the murder of Fred Bloggs?' The character in the 'hot seat' must then respond to this and the following questions. You will be amazed at how quickly the character and the scenario take shape!

- *The 'Judgement Chair'*: This is another drama technique that will help you invent rounded and interesting characters. Again, it can also be used for questioning characters that already exist in a text you are studying. It could also be used to study topics to do with citizenship or PSHE issues such as teenage pregnancy or drug abuse. A volunteer sits in the 'Judgement Chair', and then various other characters from that person's life come up to pass judgement on them. The volunteer may respond to the judgements, if they feel it is appropriate, or they might simply listen to what is said. For instance, you might use the scenario of a child who has been caught shoplifting. The characters judging the child could include their parents, brothers and sisters, police officers, teachers, etc. The parents might come up to the volunteer and say 'How could you do this to us? We're so disappointed in you ...' and so on.

- *What do I need to know?*: When creating new characters, encourage your children to invent a whole range of background information for the people they make up. This information could come under various categories, for instance physical, social, psychological, emotional. Some of the things they might need to know include: what the character looks like, what they wear, who their parents are, what job they do, what makes them angry, what makes them happy, what they like to spend their money on, etc. Your students could simply create a list of 'facts' about their character, or they could write about them in the form of an interview (perhaps with a partner asking the questions).

Show, don't tell

A classic mistake that many writers make in their fiction is to *tell* the reader what is happening, rather than *showing* them. In fact, this is often how young children first write their stories: 'Anna was sad, she was sad because she lost her teddy', and so on. In fact, you will find advice about this aspect of writing in most books for prospective novelists, but what exactly does it mean, and why is it 'wrong' to tell rather than to show?

The ideal situation when writing is for there to be nothing that intrudes between the reader and what they are reading, nothing that 'breaks the spell' of the text. When the writer *tells* the reader what is happening in their story, this creates an authorial intrusion which immediately lessens the strength of the piece of fiction. Instead of allowing the reader to work things out alone, the writer feels the need to explain what the characters are thinking and feeling. For instance, a writer who is 'telling' might say 'Shami was really angry', informing the reader about exactly what Shami's feelings are. However, a writer who is 'showing' might say 'Shami clenched her fists and a dark look came over her face.'

This distinction might seem quite small at first glance. However, showing rather than telling is important for several reasons.

- *Encouraging empathy*: Showing invites the reader to step into the character's shoes, to empathize totally with them, perhaps even 'becoming' that person while he or she is reading. It is this empathy that we are talking about when we say we became 'lost' in a book, that it was so engrossing that we forgot all about the real world.
- *Treating the reader right*: By showing rather than telling, the writer also makes an assumption about his or her readers – that they are intelligent and interested enough to work out the characters' emotions for themselves, rather than needing to be held by the hand and told.

- *Quality of writing*: Showing encourages a more visual, detailed writing style, because the writer is forced to describe the characters and what they do in detail, rather than using blunt phrases such as 'she was sad/angry/happy'. It also tends to create a style with more energy and pace, rather than a series of plodding 'facts', as you will see in the examples given below.
- *Quality of characterization*: Similarly, the writer is encouraged to create more realistic, believable characters. The student has to work out how the character might behave if she were angry, what mannerisms or actions she might use, and so on.

If we think about the way in which the best stories work, it is because the reader can visualize the people and events in his or her imagination. We see the story happening before our eyes, and this allows us to empathize with the characters, drawing us into the story. So, we have no need for the author to tell us what the characters are thinking and feeling – we know already, because we 'see' them in our heads. The following two examples point up the difference between 'telling' and 'showing' the reader.

Example 1: 'Telling' the reader
Julie was very sad. She knew that she didn't have any friends. This made her feel terrible, and she hated going to school each day. She knew that Katie and Emma hated her most of all. She felt like hitting Emma. It was all Emma's fault, but what could Julie do about it?

Example 2: 'Showing' the reader
A tear trickled down Julie's cheek. 'I'm not going to school,' she told her mum.
   'Oh yes you are,' her mum replied.
   A bitter knot of resentment pulled at Julie's stomach as she tugged on her school uniform. Dashing the tears from her cheeks, she thought back to what had happened in the playground the day before.

> 'You're not playing with us,' Katie said, Emma standing behind her, a twisted smile on her face.
>
> Julie clenched her fists hard, her fingernails biting into her palms, her head swimming with thoughts of revenge.

Narrative voice and viewpoint

In Chapter 3 we looked briefly at viewpoint, noting that it is essential to establish where the writer stands in relation to the reader before beginning work on a piece of writing. Perhaps nowhere is this more important than when writing a story. It is vital to understand both where you stand as a writer in relation to your readers and also where you stand in relation to your characters. The 'narrative voice' will be defined by the viewpoint of the writer (i.e. the person who is narrating the story). There are three 'basic' narrative voices, which are outlined below, along with some of the different effects they might create within a story.

- *First-person viewpoint*: In this viewpoint, the story is told from the perspective of the first person, using 'I' as the narrative voice. The person speaking might be one of the characters in the story, or it could be the voice of the writer. This narrative voice encourages the reader to associate strongly with the character telling the story, as we see events from their perspective. However, the writer cannot include events that his or her narrator does not directly experience.
- *Third-person viewpoint*: With this viewpoint, the story is told from a third person perspective, using 'she' or 'he'. Stories which use the third person are usually told from the viewpoint of one character, with the writer allowing us access to the thoughts and feelings of this one person. Sometimes, however, two or more characters may be used. This viewpoint does not create such a strong sense of empathy, as the reader is not viewing the story through the eyes of one person. However, the writer can describe events outside the direct experience of his or her characters.
- *Omniscient viewpoint*: In this viewpoint the writer assumes a 'godlike' position, overseeing everything in the story. The writer uses the third-person perspectives of all or most of the

different characters, and allows the reader access to their thoughts and feelings. This narrative voice is not, however, used very often in modern stories. The omniscient narrator can view and comment on everything that takes place in the story. When this style is used, however, the voice of the writer can feel quite intrusive, and perhaps because of this it tends not to appeal to modern readers.

Dialogue

We might think that writing dialogue should be the easiest thing in the world. After all, we spend our lives communicating through speech. Surely all we need to do is to turn our spoken words into written ones? However, there is much more to writing interesting and exciting dialogue than simply transferring speech onto the page. Here are some tips about how you can encourage your students to write imaginative and effective speech for the characters in their stories. Many of these ideas also apply when writing a play-script.

- *Conflict, conflict, conflict*: As you will see below ('The importance of conflict'), conflict is a vital aspect in any good piece of fiction. The need for conflict is also a crucial part of writing good dialogue, and it helps you avoid the dreary 'what did you have for breakfast?' type of speech (see Example 1 below). Some ways that you might inject conflict into dialogue include the following:
  - *Conflicting agendas*: where one character wants the opposite to the other, and each is fighting for their own position.
  - *Blocking*: where one person is refusing to agree with what the other says, and is throwing up a series of complaints or issues.
  - *Conflicting personalities*: where each character has a very different personality to the other, for instance one person is easily angered, while the other refuses to rise to the bait.
- *Avoiding boredom*: Carrying on from the point above, much of what we say in everyday life is entirely lacking in conflict. However, when we write a story, we need to find some way

of engrossing the reader, otherwise they will simply stop reading. One useful way of avoiding boredom is to twist what might have been a normal conversation into something a little more exciting, for instance by including details that are specific to the characters involved. In the examples below you will see how a mundane conversation about the time can be turned into something altogether more interesting.

- *Twisting the words*: Of course, what we say and what we mean can be two very different things. There is often a subtext going on behind our words, and this makes things more interesting for the reader. Encourage your students to play with dialogue and meaning, to have their characters saying one thing while meaning something else, or misinterpreting what the other person says.

- *Learning to listen*: Encourage your students to listen to the speech that surrounds them, for instance the conversations that they might overhear on the bus in the morning. You could set this activity as a homework task, perhaps asking them to make a note of three unusual or interesting lines of dialogue that they overhear during the course of a day, and then building a story around these.

- *Thinking about character*: The way that we speak tells other people a lot about us, and this is as true for the characters in our stories as it is in real life. For instance, an elderly gentleman who spent his life in the army would use speech very differently to a five-year-old child on her first day at school.

- *Communicating tone*: The tone of our characters' voices can be communicated in a variety of ways. Perhaps the most tempting is to use a range of verbs and adverbs, such as 'he shouted' or 'he said angrily' (see Example 1 below). However, these dialogue 'tags' can become very intrusive for the reader, especially if a number of them are used within one section of dialogue. A better option is to try to make the words themselves and the way that they are structured hint at the tone of a character's voice. See the example below for some ideas about how you might do this.

- *The invisible 'said'*: The word 'said' is, to a large extent, 'invisible' to the reader, and it allows them to focus instead on the dialogue itself. As we have seen before, the ideal for a piece of writing is for nothing to intrude between the voice of the writer (or character) and the reader. Next time you are reading a novel, notice how the word 'said' is implied rather than used.

- *Removing the dialogue tags*: Taking it one step further, it is often possible to remove the dialogue tags such as 'said' altogether. This is especially so if there are only two characters speaking in a scene. Once it has been established who is speaking and in what order, there is no real need for any further explanation. As you will see in the second example below, this can actually be shown without even the need for the word 'said'.

Example 1: How not to write dialogue

'What time is it?' Jamie asked breathlessly.

'Half-past two,' Tara answered calmly.

'It's nearly time to go back to work then,' Jamie said with a sigh.

'Do we have to?' Tara moaned plaintively.

'Yes,' Jamie answered with finality.

Example 2: How to write dialogue

Jamie glanced at his bare wrist. 'Tara, you got the time?'

'The time for what?' She winked at him and flashed a smile.

'No, what time is it?' He tapped his wrist to indicate where a watch should have been. Tara's smile vanished.

'How the hell should I know the time, Jamie? What happened to that watch I gave you for your birthday?'

'It's ... '

'Don't tell me you've broken it already, Jamie.'

'Don't start, Tara.'

'What do you mean, "don't start"? That watch cost me a bloody fortune.'

'Why is everything about money with you, Tara?'

Setting

One of the wonderful things about fiction is that it can take place in any setting that we choose, from the mountains of Borneo to the snowy wastes of Alaska, from the streets of London to a spaceship on a mission to Mars. Writers are often encouraged to 'write about what you know'. However, although our students might not have had the opportunity to travel abroad, most of them will have had ample opportunity to see other places and lives on the television. In addition, there is, of course, always room for them to use their imaginations.

As we have already seen, the most inspiring and motivating ideas for children tend to be those that are unusual. For instance, when you are setting up the classroom for some creative writing, you could turn your whole room or one part of it into 'another place'. You might use the setting of a haunted house, blacking out your room and adding some spooky sound effects, as suggested previously. Alternatively, for a story about Native American Indians, you might help create the setting by asking your class to act as a 'tribe', inventing their own tribal name and rituals, and having 'pow-wows' sitting in a circle on the floor. When doing some creative writing, why not bring in other aspects of the curriculum? For instance, when working on a science fiction story, your children could draw or paint what the surface of their alien planet looks like.

The importance of conflict

A story without conflict is boring – if the character does not face any problems or difficulties in their fictional journey, then the reader has no reason to become involved in the story. Conflict adds tension for the reader – we become caught up in the story because we are worried for the characters, fearful that they might be in danger of some kind. Adding conflict to a story makes the difference between a dull piece of writing and an interesting one. To give an example, a writer who does not utilize conflict might tell a story where Fred gets up in the morning, goes to school, comes home, does his homework and goes to bed. On the other hand, a writer who uses conflict to engage and interest us might have Fred getting up in the morning and overhearing his parents having a huge quarrel. Alternatively, Fred might arrive at school to find that aliens have taken over his world, and he is the only one who realizes. At once, the reader is engaged and wants an answer to the question 'what happens next?'

So, learning to include conflict in stories is one of the fundamental lessons of good fiction-writing. Books on writing tell us that there are three basic conflicts: person against person, person against nature, and person against him- or herself. Here are some ideas for different ways of introducing conflict, and consequently tension, into a story.

- *Problems*: Readers instinctively engage with a character who is experiencing problems of some type, because they want to know what is going to happen, and whether the character will overcome their problems. The story could be about a character who has problems making friends, or about someone with a medical problem that they must overcome. It could be about someone who is experiencing financial problems, or a character who faces an ethical dilemma. The problem could also be an external, physical one, for instance a character who gets lost in a storm. The more problems that a writer can throw at a character, the higher the level of conflict and tension will rise.
- *Obstacles*: Similarly, when an obstacle stands between a character and his or her goal, this creates conflict. (For instance, the classic example of *Romeo and Juliet*, in which the obstacle that the two lovers face is the hatred between the Montagues and the Capulets.) It is important that the goal is clear – that the reader realizes what the character is striving for, and how the obstacles are preventing him or her from reaching this goal.
- *Between characters*: Conflict will also arise between the protagonist and antagonist in the story, or to put it more simply, between the hero/heroine and the villain. This conflict might be apparent in the actions that they take, for instance fighting with each other, or in the dialogue between them.

Using conflict to develop a plot

Perhaps the one most crucial element of a good plot is that it is exciting, that is has conflict of some type. When we first write fiction, many of us make the mistake of limiting ourselves to our own lives. This can prove a particular problem for the very youngest writers, whose experience of the world is incomplete. So it is that you end up with the story in which we see Fred's day, in all its boring entirety, completely lacking in conflict or interest. However, we can help our children use and develop their imagination and creativity. It does not matter that they may only have experienced this imaginary world in their own heads, or through books, and through various forms of the media.

This, of course, is the great opportunity of fiction – the only limit is our imagination. We can create anyone and anything we like: from a character who flies to Jupiter, to one who scores the winning goal in the World Cup Final. The vital thing when working on fiction-writing is that we teach our children how to exercise their imaginations. Here are some ideas for helping your students to develop more exciting stories.

- *The worst thing*: Decide on a character with your children, for instance a boy who loves to play football, or a dog who is terrified of storms. Now ask them to think of some of the worst things that could happen to that character. For the boy who loves football, it could be breaking his leg, or being given a detention that means he misses a crucial match. For the scared dog, it could be that his owners shut him outside during a storm, or that he must go out into the storm to save someone. Immediately, these scenarios offer your students conflict with which to make their stories exciting.
- *You can't have it because . . .*: Conflict is created when a character is prevented from having what they want. Ask your students to think of a character who really really wants something: for instance a girl who desperately wants to go out with a boy in her class, or an astronaut who desperately wants to fly to the moon. Ask for volunteers to come to the front of the classroom and tell the class 'What I want most in the whole world is . . .' Then the rest of the class must come up with all the reasons why they can't have it. As they suggest these reasons, the volunteer could come up with ways of overcoming these obstacles.

- *A series of problems*: A single problem will cause conflict, but a series of problems (preferably rising in difficulty and danger as they progress) will cause a higher level of tension. To experiment with this, give your students a scenario (for instance, a group of children who go out on a boat), and ask them to come up with a series of problems for the characters to encounter, of increasing danger and complexity. For instance, in the scenario given, their series of problems might run as follows:
  - one of the children feels seasick
  - the map falls overboard and they get lost
  - a storm starts to brew
  - the boat springs a leak
  - they discover a hole in the lifeboat
  - the boat starts to sink
  - the storm begins to rage
  - the boat sinks and the children are thrown in the water
  - the sharks arrive!

- *The chain reaction*: In stories, one event leads to another, usually in a logical progression. This chain of events allows the reader to start guessing where the plot is going (although the clever author will always include a surprise or two along the way). Ask your students to think of a character who faces a dilemma, for instance a girl whose friends want her to shoplift with them. Now ask them to write about the possible consequences of the two decisions she might take. In one chain of events she might agree to shoplift, and consequently get caught by a store detective who calls the police. In the other chain, she might refuse to get involved and find that her friends reject her and start to bully her. At each stage in the plot where a dilemma occurs, the character will be faced with two or more choices, which dictate the progress of the story and which add conflict and interest for the reader.

The importance of dramatic tension
Dramatic tension is closely linked to conflict. Dramatic tension is what keeps the reader (or audience) 'on the edge of their seats'. It is what involves us with a story and its characters, and makes us

want to read on to find out what happens. Writers can develop dramatic tension through the use of conflict, as described above. However, tension can also be produced in other ways.

- *Vocabulary*: The type of words used when writing a story can be very effective in creating and developing dramatic tension, especially within certain genres. For instance, in a ghost-story words such as 'creak', 'howl', 'terror', 'petrified' would all help to keep the reader feeling tense and nervous.
- *Sentence structure*: The length and structure of sentences can also add to the level of tension created, and it is worthwhile studying examples from the thriller or action genres to see how this works. Writers will often use a series of very short sentences to create a feeling of breathy, nervous tension.
- *Imagery*: Similes, metaphors and other images can be used to great effect when adding tension to a story. The images that a writer employs may hint at danger below the surface, as in the example below, where the gargoyles have 'faces like demons', clearly suggesting that evil is in the air. Images connected to darkness and the night also give a sense that danger is all around.
- *Lighting and 'special effects'*: The best stories often have a cinematic feel to them, and when we think about films that are full of tension, there is often much use made of lighting and other special effects. It could be that darkness is used to hide the danger that lurks all around, or that a mist suddenly descends on a group of children as they walk through the forest.
- *Sound effects*: Similarly, when watching scary or tense films, sounds will often be used to add to the tension. In the example below, notice how the sound that Danny hears adds to the frightening atmosphere.
- *Character responses*: The way that a character responds to a situation will also help create tension. The reader senses the fear that the character is feeling, for instance when Danny shivers in the example below, this heightens the feeling that danger is close by.
- *The 'cliffhanger'*: A cliffhanger is often found at the end of chapters in novels, but can also be used in shorter stories.

The cliffhanger simply leaves the reader 'hanging' in the air, wondering 'what did happen next?' Sometimes their question is answered, sometimes the writer jumps to a later point in the story, leaving the reader's question unresolved.

- *Enclosed spaces*: Tension is often at its greatest when we are confined or restricted in some way. For instance, if a lift gets stuck between floors there is the opportunity for tension to rise (especially if one of the characters in the lift is claustrophobic, or has some other sort of pressing problem, such as an urgent appointment). Similarly, your characters might get trapped in a tunnel, and this too would create a high level of tension.

- *Story questions*: A story question occurs when the reader notices something within the story that seems to be significant. Within the reader's mind, he or she thinks 'Aha! I spotted something important!', and this increases the sense of involvement. For instance, the writer might mention in passing an object that later turns out to be a clue to the murderer's identity. In the example below, we hear of 'that case in '92', which is mentioned only in passing, but which is clearly going to be significant in the story.

The following example shows how some of these ideas can work together to create a high level of tension. I have used the supernatural genre, as this naturally lends itself to a feeling of danger and fear.

Danny looked up at the dark stone castle, just visible in the deepening gloom. Gargoyles hung from the battlements, their faces like demons, watching him, laughing at him. A cold wind swept down from the distant mountains and made him shiver. He pulled his coat tighter and tried to stop shaking. They had dared him to do this. To go inside. Inside the Castle of Terror. That was what they had called it. He laughed at them when they said that. 'Don't believe in the supernatural, then Dan?' Johnny asked. Dan laughed again. 'Nah, it's rubbish,' he answered, but with a rising sense of dread. 'Dare yeh to spend the night in there, then,' Johnny challenged him. Well, he could not turn back now. He had no choice. And besides he didn't believe in the supernatural. It was all a load of rubbish.

Suddenly there was a hideous sound, half scream, half moan. Danny spun around. The sound had come from behind him. From the forest. Out of the blackness. He could make out something moving towards him through the mist. He turned back to the building. What should he do? Go into the Castle of Terror? Stay out here? 'It's just Johnny trying to scare me,' he told himself. But as he turned back to the creature, and saw what it was, a scream escaped from his mouth. It was the last sound he ever made.

'We got us a body here, Jim,' the policeman spoke into his radio. 'Looks like some maniac on the loose. Bad injuries, ain't seen nothing this nasty in a long, long time. Not since, you know, that case in '92. You better get the forensics team out here right away.'

Writing scripts

There are a number of differences between writing a script and writing a story, and it is important for students to understand this before they attempt to write scenes or plays of their own. When they first write a script, many children will use a narrator to describe the events that are taking place. Rather than this being a deliberate choice, it tends to be because they are inexperienced in telling a story through dialogue, and by resorting to a narrator they can put across the action by *telling* the audience what is happening, rather than *showing* them this through what the characters say and do. (See the earlier section in this chapter, 'Show, don't tell' (p. 101), for some more thoughts on this problem.)

The section in this chapter on dialogue will give you some ideas about writing effective speech, and these apply just as readily to scripts as to stories or novels. When writing scripts, do take the time to talk through with your students about exactly what makes this particular form of writing special. Here are some ideas that you might like to consider.

- *Audience*: A script is written to be performed rather than read. Scripts are aimed at a 'live' audience (whether in a theatre, watching a television show or film), rather than a reader sitting with a book. When writing scripts, this should be taken into account. Encourage your students to visualize their scripts being performed rather than viewing them as static dialogue on the page. In fact, some of the best scripts come out of practical work – improvisations in which the storyline and characters gradually appear, and which are then put down on paper.
- *Characters*: In a script (or play), we learn about the characters through the things that they say and do, and the way that they appear. This means that the dialogue alone must show us what these people are like. The writer might also include stage directions to show the director or actors how the lines should be spoken.
- *Plot*: Similarly, the audience can only understand the plot through the words and actions of the characters. Stage directions may be used to explain the location of the events, but these should be shown through the onstage setting, rather than by a narrator who gives this information to the audience.
- *Layout*: Before working on scriptwriting, it is important for the teacher to show students how a script should be laid out. This will include information such as not using speech-marks, how to give stage directions, and so on.

Writing poetry

In my experience, younger children respond well to poetry, and really enjoy writing poems of their own. However, by the time students get into the later years of secondary school (or even before this age) some of them have been 'turned off' the whole idea of poetry as a form for writing. For this reason, as well as talking about general approaches to teaching poetry in this section, I have also included some ideas for teachers who are finding poetry difficult to teach, whether because of poor class behaviour or lack of interest.

First approaches to poetry

When approaching poetry-writing, I would recommend that you start off by digging into exactly what does make a poem a poem. This is actually surprisingly hard to ascertain. After all, both poetry and prose might include imagery, words that rhyme, rhythmic language, sensory perceptions, and so on. At its heart, a poem is a piece of condensed language, one which creates a strong image or a series of pictures. In addition, poetry is essentially about sound and rhythm, about the way that words sound when they are spoken out loud. However, even these descriptions do not fit all poems. Here are some questions that you might like to raise with your class.

- What is the difference between a poem and a song?
- If we listen to a song without music, is it a poem?
- Do all poems have to rhyme?
- What is the difference between a non-rhyming poem and a piece of prose?
- How are poems laid out on the page?
- Do all poems tell a story?
- Do all poems have to 'make sense'?
- What makes a good poem?
- Are poems designed to be read on the page, spoken out loud, or both?

Inspirations for poetry

Finding a powerful and engaging inspiration is often the key to success in motivating your children to create their own poetry. The following ideas should give you some ways into writing poems, both for young, emerging writers and for older, more experienced students.

- *Events*: When something important or moving happens, writing poetry can be a good way of dealing with our responses. Writing poems provides an excellent way to express our feelings, to turn our emotions into words. For this reason, poetry may be effective when dealing with PHSE and citizenship issues within the classroom.
- *Places*: Because of its generally descriptive nature, poetry

offers an effective format for creating a 'sense of place', a 'word-picture' that captures a particular setting. You might ask your students to use their senses to brainstorm the sounds, scents, images, and so on, that they associate with a particular place. You could also use poetry as part of the response after a trip to somewhere inspiring.

- *People*: Poetry offers an excellent form for describing a character in detail. Children today live in a celebrity-obsessed world, so why not ask them to turn their knowledge about their favourite famous person into a poem? This subject will certainly act as an excellent motivator. Alternatively, they might write a poem about someone they know well, perhaps their best friend, parent, or even (if you're feeling brave) their teacher.

- *Objects*: Just as an artist looks deeply at an object before and during the act of drawing it, so a poet can study something in detail with words. As we have already seen, children can be inspired by a teacher who brings a 'thing' into the classroom, the more unusual the better. When using an object for inspiration, you might start the lesson with a brainstorm of all the sensory words associated with it, as well as possible narratives connected to the object.

- *Other poets' work*: When approaching a particular topic in poetry, a good way into the work is to show your class samples of work by other poets on that subject. For instance, when introducing war poetry, we might read poems by Wilfred Owen, Siegfried Sassoon, and so on.

The process of poetry

Because of its nature, writing poetry is as much about the process of writing as it is about the finished product. It can take longer to find inspiration for and to edit a poem effectively than it does to actually write the piece itself. It is tempting for children to write a poem and declare it 'finished' without undergoing the processes that lead to a really powerful piece of work. However, if you can encourage your students to spend time working and reworking their poems, they will not only end up with a better finished product, but they will also be practising some of the most important writing skills. Here are some suggestions about how you might prepare your children before they get down to the actual writing of a poem, and how you can encourage them to work and rework the piece once it is underway.

- *Brainstorming*: The brainstorm is almost tailor-made for the poetry-writer, because it encourages us to pick out single striking images that may prove useful in the writing. For instance, a brainstorm on the word 'black cat' might bring out images to do with how the cat moves, looks and sounds. It might also inspire your students to think of other associations, such as witches, darkness and night.
- *The senses*: Good poetry engages all the reader's senses. When you have found a topic for your children to work with, encourage them to think about how each of their senses might be involved. A good way to do this is to use a senses' worksheet (see 'Using your senses', p. 96, earlier in this chapter).
- *Sound*: As well as simply reading the words on the page (whether in the 'finished' poem or in the initial drafts), encourage your children to think about the sounds that their poetry is making and to read their work out loud. This might involve exploring alliterative effects within the piece, or it might be about onomatopoeic words and the impact that they have.
- *Cutting*: In some cases, the fewer words a poem has, the better and stronger the image it creates. When your children have 'finished' their piece, ask them to count the number of words that it has. Now tell them to cut that number of words exactly in half, as in the stream of consciousness exercise described earlier (see 'Warm-up exercises' in Chapter 1, p. 12). This cutting process might not lead to a 'better' poem, but it encourages the children to think about which words are vital and which can be dropped.
- *Structure*: When editing poetry, encourage your children to think about the way in which the piece is structured, as well as the words it contains. This might involve dividing a poem up into verses, or laying it out in an interesting way on the page.

Motivating those who 'don't do' poetry

It is a pity that there are some students who just, 'don't do' poetry, whether writing it or reading it. After all, 99.9 per cent of modern-day children love popular music, and what else is a song but poetry put to music? I think this is the connection we are missing – a way of making poetry relevant to their everyday lives, rather than seeing it as something 'literary' and perhaps rather middle class. So, here are some thoughts about how you can motivate and engage those who believe that they have no interest in poems.

- *Appealing themes*: When working with poorly motivated students, try to find a theme or topic that is going to appeal. For instance, I once taught a class of GCSE students who were poorly motivated when it came to poetry. There was a high percentage of boys in the class, and it was important to find some way of engaging their interest. To do this, I used a variety of poems on the subject of football, which caught their attention and proved highly motivating for them.
- *Well-known poems*: Similarly, students also engage with poems that they know well or that they associate with a different medium, such as film. For instance, the poem 'Stop All the Clocks', by W.H. Auden, appeared in the film *Four Weddings and a Funeral*. When using this poem to inspire my students, I have found that they are pleased at the fact that they already know the poem.
- *Topics close to their hearts*: When trying to motivate your students, try to pick a topic that is important to them. Depending on their ages, this could be starting at school, first love, families, and so on.
- *Appealing forms*: There is a great deal of what we would traditionally call poetry in modern-day musical forms, such as rap and hip-hop. These musical styles rely on the spoken word, with a strong rhythmical feel, and you can use this connection within the classroom as a motivator. For instance, I have used the whole idea of rapping very effectively in the classroom, 'rapping' iambic pentameter with a class who were studying *Romeo and Juliet*, adding a beat by tapping on the desks.

- *Songs as poetry*: Many songs can, with their lyrics typed out, be presented as 'poetry'. I once used this idea for a language-analysis lesson, in which I began by analysing the 'poems' (lyrics) with the class, and then went on to show that these poems were in fact songs. We explored the tone of the poems as written pieces, and then looked at the way in which the music fitted (or didn't fit) the tone we had identified. This work could be followed up by asking your students to bring in songs of their own choice for inspiration and analysis.

- *Something shocking*: I will leave you to decide how far you are willing to go (depending a great deal on your school and the particular age of children that you teach) in employing 'shock tactics'. However, suffice to say that there are plenty of 'shocking' poems out there (both in terms of subject and language) that might well motivate students who are bored by conventional poetry.

- *Pure analysis*: Sometimes the least well-motivated children are engaged by the feeling that they are learning something highly technical and analytical. If this is the case with your class, introduce them to the delights of extended metaphors, pathetic fallacy, assonance, alliteration, and so on. You may well find that they surprise you in their level of interest.

6 Non-fiction writing

This chapter introduces you to a range of strategies and ideas for working on non-fiction writing. I use the term 'non-fiction' to refer to the form of the writing (instruction booklets, newspapers, and so on) as opposed to the content of or inspiration for the writing. In many of the examples here, I use a creative basis for the content, but ask the students to write *as though* this imaginary content is factual. Of course, non-fiction writing crops up in practically every area of the curriculum and I hope that teachers from whatever subject background will find some new ideas from this chapter to try in their own classrooms.

Taking notes

I have put this section right at the start of the chapter, because for much non-fiction writing, our students need to do research and take notes before they can start work. In addition, learning to take notes from a teacher giving information orally plays an important role in learning for older students. Taking notes is all about identifying the most important pieces of information, and then finding some way of writing these down so that they will be accessible at a later stage. This vital skill can, however, be an area of real weakness for some children, and it is something that we need to train our students to do properly. Below are some ideas about how you might develop this skill with your classes.

- *Practise scanning texts*: Learning to skim or speed read texts is a very useful part of taking notes. One exercise to develop this skill is to give your students a very limited time to read through a page of text, time that they must use to pick out only the most important words. This forces them to utilize their visual reading ability, rather than spending time sounding out each individual word. Your children may surprise themselves at how straightforward this scanning is to do, and with practice it becomes ever easier.

- *Practise annotating texts*: Annotation is closely related to note-taking, because when we annotate we are identifying important words or phrases, underlining or highlighting them, and showing why they are important. The skill of annotation can be taught at an early age, using the very simplest texts, then revisited again and again as the students move higher up the school.

- *Work with listening as well as reading*: As well as taking notes from written texts, you should also train your students to take notes from an oral source. For instance, you might read a story to your class and ask them to make short notes about the important events and characters.

- *Work with an overhead projector*: Seeing the teacher annotating or making notes on an overhead projector or electronic whiteboard will help the students learn this skill. As mentioned in Chapter 1, seeing their teacher as a 'writer' is also a very important part of motivating our children.

- *Use a concise and relevant layout*: Teach your children too about how notes can be written in a way that makes them easy to access in the future. For instance, they might use a series of brainstorms to note facts on each topic area.

- *Use colours*: As well as using a form of layout such as the brainstorm, your students might also use different colours for different subject areas within their notes.

Building your writing

A large part of the process of 'writing' my books, actually involves 'building' them, and this approach is especially effective when working with non-fiction. I start with an outline of what the book might include, and only gradually is this outline filled in and the book completed. For many students, the temptation is to view writing in the same way that they experience reading – to start at the beginning of a text and to move forwards until they get to the end. However, there is a huge difference between reading a finished piece of text and creating your own writing. The writer of the text you are reading will, of course, have spent a substantial amount of time following at least some of the vital steps described in Chapter 3, and this is ideally what you want to encourage your students to do too. This approach to writing is especially helpful for your students when they are using computers for written work, which makes the process much simpler (see Chapter 11).

To give a metaphorical example, building your writing is much the same as building a house. You start with the 'big picture', the overall design of the piece, and then gradually construct the frame and begin to add the walls. It is only when the building is complete that the 'finishing touches' can be added. In the same way, I might first approach a piece of writing with an initial idea or overall plan, then move on to add chapter headings, section headings, and so on. At this stage the writing itself might start, with time spent elaborating each section in turn and perhaps reordering or restructuring the overall shape of the piece. Finally, I would look through the completed text of a book to 'tidy up' and make the smaller linguistic changes and corrections that finish off the work. Here is a more detailed explanation of how you might get your students to 'build' their writing, using some of the processes described in Chapter 3. An interesting way of approaching this activity with your students could be to use the metaphor described above of building a house.

Building a house	Building a piece of writing
Select the type of house and its location	Select a form for the writing
Know who you are building it for	Know your audience
Think about the style of the house	Think about the style of your writing
Come up with initial ideas	Brainstorm your ideas
Find out technical details	Research facts/information
Make an initial design	Map your ideas/points
Decide on building materials	Select your material
Make a detailed design	Plan your writing

Build the foundations	Build your initial outline
Put up the main structure	Add in details of each section
Build the walls	Start to build the writing
Put on the roof and lay floors	Sort out the introduction/ conclusion
Work on the interiors	Edit and rework the writing and structure
Finalize the decorations	Sort out technical and stylistic touches

Non-fiction forms

When writing factual pieces, for instance in history, geography, science, etc., there is no reason at all why we should not be inventive with the forms that we use, especially if we need to motivate our students. For instance, on occasions you might use the newspaper form to write about a historical event, or the recipe form to write out a chemistry experiment. Here is a list of some different forms that have the potential to be used in non-fiction writing across the curriculum:

- summaries
- newspaper stories
- reviews
- reports
- detailed analysis
- essays
- brochures and pamphlets
- programmes
- manuals
- instruction booklets
- recipes
- shopping lists
- letters
- emails
- web pages
- diaries
- news reports

- police reports
- witness statements
- TV programmes
- magazines, including:
  - articles
  - problem pages
  - letters pages
  - advertisements.

Frames and structures

The Literacy Strategy encourages us to offer our students 'frames' for their work, and this is an excellent idea, especially for the less able, as it helps them to structure their writing. When working with these frames or structures, try to get your children to identify the features for themselves, rather than always providing them with a ready-made framework. This will create a sense of ownership of the ideas, and will also help to develop their analytical skills. For instance, you might look at a series of letters with your students, identifying the aspects and features that appear in each one, and then applying these to the children's own work. Similarly, you might read a number of recipes with your class and explore the way in which they are structured, and the elements that must be included. These details could be brainstormed in groups, then annotated on an overhead projector or board for the whole class to use.

Technique and non-fiction writing

Of course, technique is just as important when writing a piece of non-fiction as it is when doing 'creative' writing. The word technique might apply to the accuracy of the work in terms of its spelling, punctuation and grammar, but it might also apply to the technique involved in structuring a piece of writing, or in drafting and editing the work. There is much information earlier in this book about technique: ideas about the basics in Chapter 2, thoughts on developing writing techniques throughout the process in Chapter 3, and strategies for effective essay-writing in Chapter 4. When you are working on non-fiction writing, do consider the ideas given in these chapters, as well as the more 'creative' approaches described in Chapter 5.

Rhythm

The technique of giving 'rhythm' to our writing can make the difference between an average and a good piece of work, between a piece of writing that is stilted or uneven, and one that seems to 'flow' and 'sounds right'. Although rhythm is something we traditionally associate with poetry, all good writing has an internal rhythm of its own, and this is just as true for non-fiction as it is for 'creative' writing. This is an area that you might like to explore when working on non-fiction pieces with your students, whether you are working with the youngest writers or the oldest. The rhythm of our writing is made up a range of components: the sound and length of the words that we use; the way that we structure our sentences and paragraphs; the type of connecting words that we use, and so on. Here are some thoughts about this aspect of writing, and how you might develop your own students' use of rhythm.

- *'Hearing' the writing*: When we explore the rhythm of our writing, we need to be able to 'hear' it. This could be done by reading the work out loud, perhaps to the class or to a partner. However, it might also be done by developing the internal voice that 'speaks' to us as we write. In fact, it is important to help your children develop this internal voice, because when they are writing in exams they will not be able to 'hear' their writing out loud.
- *Developing grammatical structures*: If you are working with emerging writers, those who are just learning to put their words down on the page, you may well notice how 'stilted' their writing sounds. Because they have a limited vocabulary and understanding of technique, they tend to use sentences with a basic single-clause structure of subject–verb–object. For instance, 'The girl / threw / the ball.' It is only as they develop an understanding of more complex grammatical structures (either in their speech, their writing or their reading) that the writing can start to flow.
- *Mixing sentence lengths*: A piece of writing with a good

rhythm will generally have mixed sentence lengths. Short sentences might be used to develop tension or pace, or to give the piece a feeling of simplicity and clarity. There is sometimes a tendency to write a long sentence that would in fact be better expressed as a couple of shorter ones. When you are working with your children on the rhythm of their writing, ask them to consider whether they can 'break down' some of their sentences into shorter, more pithy ones.

- *'Notate' the writing*: When we are analysing the rhythm or metre of poetry, we break down each line into syllables and stresses. We can also do this with narrative or non-fiction writing, for instance counting the number of words and syllables in each sentence, to identify the rhythm that we are using. These could even be written out like a musical score, to explore the overall pattern. Certain words will also create a strong emphasis within a sentence, and this is also true of presentational devices such as italic and bold.

Tone

The tone required for a piece of non-fiction writing depends a great deal on the reason behind the writing, and the audience that is being addressed. Even if you view your subject area as completely factual, your students will still need to consider the tone in which they write, if they are to develop their writing beyond the average. Being able to write with a 'tone' is closely connected to finding our own 'voice' (see above) and the ability to 'hear' ourselves when we write. For instance, when writing to complain about something, we might sound indignant or shocked. When writing to instruct we may use a calm, unemotional tone of voice. There are various ways in which we can 'add' tone into our writing. Here are just a few ideas.

- *The use of questions*: A question, especially within a piece of non-fiction writing, creates a very particular tone. The question might be rhetorical, or it might be a direct question to the reader/audience. It might be asked with a horrified tone, or as a simple query. Using questions tends to slow down or pause the reader, as they consider what their own answer would be. Using questions also creates a strong connection between writer and reader, as the writer is, in effect, directly addressing his or her audience.

- *The use of statements*: Making statements should always be done with care in non-fiction writing, especially if the subject being discussed is a controversial one, or is not generally considered as 'fact' (see Chapter 4 for some ideas on how to write 'interpretive' statements). The overuse of statements can create quite a pompous tone, as though the writer believes that what he or she says is always right and definitive. Encourage your students to experiment with making interpretations rather than statements. This will help them both in creating tone in their writing, and also in those awkward examination moments when they are unsure if what they are writing is 100 per cent correct.

- *Use of italic/bold*: Putting a word or phrase in italic or bold can create a strong and emphatic tone. However, these presentational devices should be used sparingly, rather than being scattered throughout the writing. In fact, a writer with a strong sense of 'voice' may be able to suggest emphasis simply through the words and structures used.

The importance of being an expert

When we are writing a factual or non-fiction piece, we have the opportunity to play the role of an 'expert'. The level of actual expertise that we have will vary considerably, depending on our age, the subject involved and our level of personal knowledge. However, in my experience there is something wonderfully motivational about playing this particular role, and nowhere is this more so than when working with children. By creating the fiction that your students are in fact a group of experts on a particular subject, and giving them the power that goes along with this role, you will find amazing levels of motivation can be achieved. The students love being taken 'out of' the school setting and put into a fictional scenario in which they have power and influence. Once again, we are setting up a 'fiction' within the classroom, allowing our students to feel that they are removed from the day-to-day school setting and instead being given a role to play. Their enthusiasm will often lead to them researching deeply into a subject, so that they can live up to their positions as 'experts'.

When using the role of experts for non-fiction writing, I have found that one of the best approaches is to use a group project, in which the students work together as experts in a particular field. This allows each member of the group to utilize their own particular abilities and talents, and also to learn from the people that they are working with. I have used this type of 'experts project' with great success when working with targeted, lower-ability groups, as well as with the more able. The following two sections give you some thoughts about how you can set up a group project of your own, and some ideas about potential 'fictions' for this non-fiction writing.

Running a group project

Before setting up and running a group project, there are various technical and organizational issues that you should address. The points below are ones that I have learned from the experience of actually using these projects within my classroom. It is well worth spending the time to consider the practical concerns that might arise before you begin work on a group project of your own.

- *Group numbers*: The best number for a group project is generally about four students. Much more than this, and the groups will find it hard to work together and to keep themselves organized. Less than this, and you will miss out on the different areas of skill that each student brings to the work. You might find that some of your students want to work in pairs, and it is up to you to decide whether you feel that this is acceptable.
- *Group mixes*: Group projects offer us an excellent opportunity for mixed ability work. The more able and the 'leaders' in the group will tend to help out their less able or less forceful counterparts.
- *Choice of groups*: Students tend to work best if they choose their own groups, working with people that they like. If you allow your children to choose the make-up of their groups, make sure that some of the less popular or quieter children are not left out.

- *Timescale*: I have found that it is important to set a time-scale before beginning this type of work. Otherwise, the work tends to expand to fit the amount of time you are willing to give it. Far better to set a realistic timescale and then give your class targets for the amount of work they must complete in each lesson.

- *Setting the focus*: In order to keep your children 'on task', it is a good idea to write out a worksheet that gives them a series of activities to complete. These can then be divided up within the group.

- *Keeping the focus*: It can be tempting for students to lose their focus, and to spend excessive amounts of time on an area of the project that they particularly enjoy. To avoid this problem, you could ask your children to set themselves specific tasks to complete during each lesson, and also to set themselves homework tasks.

- *Audience*: For most of the projects suggested below, there will be a specific audience for the work. If you can make the audience as 'real' as possible, for instance selling the magazine to other students within the school, this will help motivate your children to produce their best possible work.

- *Presentation*: If at all possible, do give your students the opportunity to present at least some of their work on the computer. This will help them to produce a 'finished product' of some type.

Ideas for group projects

Below are some suggestions for group projects that allow your students to become experts, whether they are five or fifteen years old, and in various areas of the curriculum. Many are media-related. In my experience, as well as enjoying the idea of being an 'expert', working on projects in this way can be a very engaging experience because it allows each child to offer his or her own strengths, talents and opinions to the group. Boys seem to respond particularly well to this type of work.

- *The personnel managers' dilemma*: I have used this exercise with a range of classes, from the 'easy' to the 'highly challenging'. In every case I have found it to be very successful. The basic format of the lesson is that the students are personnel managers, and they have to decide how to save money for their company. This might be achieved by sacking some staff, or in another, more lateral way (it's up to them how they do it.) The groups are given a list of staff, with details about their work backgrounds, experience, qualifications, home life, and so on. They must then consult together, writing a report on their findings, and presenting their ideas to the class. I have used this activity in English lessons, but it could also prove useful for business studies, maths or citizenship work.

- *The pop group*: Again, a highly successful project, even with poorly motivated students. The students work in a group, playing the role of the managers of a pop group. They must work on a range of different tasks for their group: from writing song lyrics to making a CD cover, from designing posters for the tour to writing a fanzine for the band.

- *The football team*: Similarly, for this project members of the group work as managers of a football team. Again, they must write in a variety of forms for their team. For instance, they design and label a home and away team kit, they write and produce a match programme, and so on.

- *The magazine*: For many children, much of the day-to-day reading that they do will be of magazines. Boys as well as girls seem to enjoy reading magazines, on a wide range of subjects from football and music to computer games. When setting a group project to make a magazine you can choose from a huge range of different subject areas, depending which area of the curriculum you wish to focus on.

- *The time-travellers*: For work in history, you might tell your students that they are experts who can travel back to a specific point in time, for instance the date of a significant historical event. You could ask them to research the situation in which they find themselves, and then make a written report to the class on the situation and conditions at that point in history. This report might be in a range of non-fiction forms, from the diary to the newspaper article, and so on. (This work can be complemented nicely by watching the film *Bill and Ted's Excellent Adventure*.)

- *Volcano*: In a geography lesson, the children might have expertise in dealing with a particular type of phenomenon, such as a volcano, earthquake, tidal wave, environmental disaster, etc. They could be called into a situation as 'consultants', providing advice on how to deal with the problem. They might also write a report assessing their findings and advising how the people might prepare for the next time the phenomenon occurs.

Writing for a range of reasons

When working on non-fiction writing, as well as considering the form in which you will ask your students to write, you also need to think about the reason behind the writing. For the least well-motivated students, telling them to write simply because they 'have to' is unlikely to lead to successful work. Giving our children a reason for their writing is a good way of motivating them, and it also sets them very clear targets to follow and aims to achieve. Thinking about *why* we are writing what we are writing also encourages us to consider the appropriate form, tone, and structure of the piece. In the following sections I have covered just three of the many different reasons why we might write non-fiction.

Writing to instruct and explain

When you are working on writing to instruct and explain, one of the main skills you will be teaching is the art of sequencing. This skill is crucial to good writing, as it helps your children learn about ordering ideas or events within any piece of writing. At the earliest age, the skill of sequencing might help with learning to give a story a beginning, middle and end (and in the appropriate order). At a later stage in their schooling, the skill of sequencing will help your students to write essays and longer pieces of fiction and non-fiction, again ordering their ideas in the most fitting order.

There is a wonderful email currently doing the rounds, entitled 'How to give a cat a pill'. The email gives a list of instructions describing the increasingly desperate (and hilarious) events as the cat's owner attempts to force a pill down the cat's throat. There are a couple of reasons why this piece of writing is so appealing. Firstly, it strikes a note of total recognition in anyone who has ever tried to give a cat a pill. Secondly, it is the escalation of increasingly outrageous events, so that by the end of the story the owner is having to extract the cat from a nearby tree, and she has to be admitted to hospital so that her own wounds can be treated!

Here are some ideas about writing to instruct and explain, which give you some original ways of approaching this area.

- *Recipes*: Recipes provide an excellent writing form for covering a variety of topics. One of the main features of a recipe is a sequence of instructions that must be followed in the correct order, in order to succeed. Use recipes in unusual or imaginative ways. You could ask your children to write a recipe for a spell, based on a reading of the witches' spell in *Macbeth* or on an extract from *Harry Potter*. Ask them to decide on a purpose for their recipe, for instance a love-potion or a spell to make their teacher do what they say. Get them to choose the most gruesome ingredients that they can think of. Another idea for using recipes is to write a recipe for their ideal teacher, which might include 2 teaspoons of laughter, a pinch of strictness, half a pound of smiles, and so on.

- *Instruction booklets*: Again, writing an instruction booklet will help your children develop the skill of sequencing. And as anyone who has ever tried to put together a piece of flat-pack furniture using the instructions will know, good instructions are not necessarily easy to write! Again, try to find an imaginative topic on which to write your instructions. You might ask your children to write instructions for 'How to make a monster', in response to reading an extract from *Frankenstein*. Or you could write a series of instructions on 'How to make your teacher angry' (if you're daring enough.)

- *Mapping*: When we are giving instructions to follow a map, or to find directions to a particular place, we need to give the instructions in the correct order. We might ask our students to write directions to a real place, but we could also offer them a fictional map, perhaps of a treasure island, and ask them to give directions about how to arrive at the treasure.

Writing to complain

Writing to complain can be great fun, as it allows us to put forward a very strong and personal point of view. It can provide the students with a good reason for their writing and, in addition, can lead to some humorous and engaging pieces of work. Generally speaking, we seem much more willing to complain nowadays: as consumers we are far more aware of our rights and also of the responsibilities that companies have towards us. Writing to complain offers some wonderful opportunities for experimenting with language and tone. Here are some thoughts, ideas and strategies that you might find useful.

- *What is my tone?*: When writing to complain, we need to find the right tone: one that is appropriate to the audience being addressed. We need not only to put across the way that we feel but also to ensure that something gets done about our problem. Again, develop the idea of 'voice' with your students – how would what I have written sound if I were saying it out loud to my reader? How would it make them feel – angry, irritated, or willing to help me?
- *A sense of purpose*: When we are writing to complain, we generally want to achieve something, whether it is for the council to fill in the holes in the road, or for a company to refund us for a faulty product. This strong sense of purpose gives a wonderful energy to the writing.
- *Complaining and vocabulary*: Writing to complain offers us the chance to use a range of words and phrases, many of which we probably wouldn't employ in our day-to-day writing. Thus children can extend their choice of vocabulary, and revel in the sound and effect of the words that they use.
- *A real purpose*: Many of us, whether we are five or fifty, feel strongly about certain issues in our lives, and letters written to complain can enable students to express themselves for a real and genuine purpose. For instance, they might write to complain about pollution in a nearby lake, or to express their concern about the proposed closure of a local swimming pool.
- *Catharsis*: Writing to complain is a wonderful way of getting our anger out over an issue. Using writing across the curriculum: in a geography lesson your students might write

to the local council to complain about pollution, or in a PE lesson to their local MP to complain about a lack of local sports facilities.

- *Working on different styles*: There is also the opportunity for work on style, tone and use of vocabulary. Why not ask your students to write the 'same' letter of complaint, but in a range of different styles, from the calm to the extremely angry? Or perhaps they could start their letter calmly, but get gradually more enraged as the writing progresses.

Writing and personal communication

Personal communication plays a hugely important role in our lives. It is a role that is constantly expanding, as a huge range of different opportunities for communicating open up to us. In the last few years, there has been an explosion in technology that has resulted in wide access to emails, text messages and the internet. (Chapter 10 gives you some more ideas about different forms of communication that are connected to the use of ICT, such as email and the internet.) Conventionally, the main form of written communication has been the letter, and this is still true today, although we might send an email or text message rather than using 'snail mail'. Traditional, formal letters use a fairly strict format, and English teachers teach the necessary form and vocabulary for these. However, newer forms of communicative writing require a different approach.

When they are writing to communicate, your students need to make certain conscious decisions that will influence their work. Here are some questions that they might like to ask themselves when writing to communicate.

- What do I want to communicate?
- What form is it most appropriate for me to communicate with?
- Who or what is the audience that I am communicating with?
- How formal does my communication need to be?
- What style of writing should I use to make my communication effective?
- What response am I hoping to receive?

Writing about writing

One of the best ways in which to develop any skill to its highest level is to watch and learn from the 'masters' at work, whether this involves studying football with a professional coach, or learning about a subject at university from academic professors. With writing, we are lucky in that we are surrounded by text in our daily lives, and we have many opportunities to explore how others write successfully. Possibly one of the best ways of developing and enhancing our own writing is to study that of others, particularly those who write professionally. Within the classroom, this might involve the study of language in various non-fiction forms, as well as the study and analysis of novels and other creative writing.

Writing about language

Analysing and writing about the way in which other writers use language helps our students to develop a greater understanding of their own work. The analysis of both simple and complex texts can teach us a great deal, and this study can begin at a very early age. For instance, with our youngest children we might explore how the instructions for a children's board game are written, whilst with older students we might look at the ways in which advertisers appeal to their market. This analysis of language use can take place across the curriculum: for example, getting your students to study the way a scientific report is written before writing one of their own.

There are various things to consider when studying and writing about language. Here are some questions that you might find useful.

- What type of audience is this piece of writing aimed at?
- What age are the audience?
- What type of people are the audience?
- How does the intended audience affect the way that the piece is written?
- What form is the writing in?
- Why has this particular form been used?
- What viewpoint is being used (i.e. first- or third-person)?
- What type of words or vocabulary are used?
- How simple or complicated is the vocabulary and sentence structure?
- How long is each word or sentence?

- Is the writing difficult or easy to understand?
- How formal or informal is the writing?
- How is the piece structured – what is in each paragraph and why?
- How does the writing start and finish?
- What point or points is the writer trying to make?
- Is the writer trying to convince us of a particular point of view? Do they succeed?
- What tone does the writer use?
- Is the writer feeling a certain emotion or mood?
- Does the writer use any linguistic devices within the piece?
- How is the piece of writing laid out on the page?
- Are there any special presentational devices used, such as different fonts?
- Do you find this piece of writing interesting or engaging? Why? Why not?
- What techniques does the writer use that you might be able to incorporate into your own writing?

Writing about literature

In the same way that studying and writing about language use can help us develop our own writing, so looking at literature in detail can be very beneficial for our creative work. The closeness of the connection between the acts of reading and writing means that even our youngest children will be able to make a simple analysis of the way that books work. By studying the way in which authors write, we can help both the youngest and the oldest students to develop their own writing.

Here are some areas of discussion that you might like to use when asking young children of about seven years old to analyse the children's books that their younger siblings might read.

- Language devices, for instance the repetition of certain phrases.
- Type of vocabulary, such as short and simple words.
- The way in which the sentences are structured.
- Use of pictures to help with understanding meaning.
- Topics or genres that will appeal to young readers.
- Colourful layout and large print.

Analysing texts

When you are thinking about 'literary' texts to use with your students, do bear in mind the advice given in Chapter 1 about motivation. Although working with 'great' literature can be a real challenge (and consequently motivational in its own right), don't forget sometimes to include texts that are topical or fun. For instance, there is no reason why we cannot analyse and write about a story in a comic book or magazine, as well as the more highbrow works. When introducing the techniques of literary study, I have had great success with extracts from books by Stephen King and Patricia Cornwell (remember, gruesome bits of description can be wonderfully gripping for children).

Asking our students to analyse and write about fiction is an excellent way of introducing them to the techniques that lie behind great writing. By 'picking apart' books in this way, and writing about them in a non-fictional context, we can show our children the complexity of 'good' fictional writing. The initial analysis of a piece of literature is also an excellent point at which to introduce the skill of annotation. For instance, at the youngest age you might simply ask children to underline words that are the same within a text, to explore the effect of repetition. With older students the annotations could include notes in the margins as well. Above all, working with 'literature' should be an active process that helps our students develop their own writing. Show your children that it's OK to pick books apart and to scribble notes on them (preferably on a photocopy, in pencil, or on their own copy of the book). That way, we can demystify the world of books, and remove some of the barriers that stand between the reluctant writer and the text.

Part 3

Writing it right

7 Writing and assessment

Most of the writing that our children do in school will of course be assessed in some way, whether it is simply marking their exercise books, keeping a record of certain pieces of work to assess their progress in class, or writing for externally assessed examinations. However, we should never consider that our students are writing *for* assessment – the writing will (or should) always have a reason, and an audience, beyond this. This chapter deals with the assessment of writing. I give some thoughts and ideas about how teachers might approach assessment and mark their students' writing in the most effective way. I also look at how we can help our students deal with their writing and its assessment in public examinations.

Increasingly, it seems, we are being asked to assess and grade our children's work from a very early age. Whilst this is not the place for a discussion of the rights and wrongs of this approach, I do feel strongly that such constant testing can erode the self-esteem of those who most need help, those for whom writing is a real struggle, and those whose motivation is low. As we mark and assess their work, we do need to fight against any potential damage that might be done to our poorly motivated students, those with special needs and the least able.

Marking writing

When we mark a piece of writing, we are effectively making a judgement, acting as both reader and reviewer of what the child has produced. This is a very powerful position to be in. Making judgements on someone else's writing needs to be done with care and sensitivity, because writing is such a personal thing, such a reflection of our own personality. Our ultimate aim, of course, should be for children to play both roles – to be able to read, review (and consequently edit) their own work, until they are happy with the end result and ready to show it to an audience. This, however, is a long-term goal that may never be reached during a child's school career.

When we do mark our students' writing, we need to think carefully about the purpose of the assessment that we are doing, about what we are actually marking *for*. In some subjects, and for some teachers, the content of the writing may be far more important than the way that the student has expressed him- or herself, or the technique that he or she has used. For other teachers (and increasingly for all teachers, with the National Literacy Strategy coming into play), judgements will have to be made about technique as well as content, with the teacher considering how well the child has actually written, in addition to the content of their work.

It is fair to say that at times, when we are overburdened with paperwork or any of the myriad pressures of our jobs, marking can become little more than a paper exercise – a job that needs to be done, but with little thought about the reasons behind it and its potential benefits. If we are honest, this type of marking (often tick and flick – see below) is perhaps meaningless, certainly almost worthless in educational terms. It is at times like these that we need to return to our original motivation for marking, which is primarily to help our students learn, to help them understand what is good and bad about their written work, and how they might improve it. Here are just some of the different ways in which marking can help in this learning process.

- Showing the child where they have made errors.
- Helping them to learn why they have made these mistakes.
- Helping them to avoid making the same mistakes again.
- Showing children what is good or effective about their work.
- Helping them learn why these particular aspects of their writing are effective.
- Helping them to repeat the effective parts of what they have written.
- Making children feel positive about their written work to help motivate them.

- Praising children for what has gone well to encourage them in the future.

Marking symbols

The technical aspects of a piece of writing can take a surprisingly long time to correct, especially if we are writing out our corrections in full. This is where marking symbols are extremely useful. By using these symbols, we can make our job as teachers faster and more efficient. Sharing these symbols with our students should also enable them to correct their own drafts more quickly and effectively.

You can find some of the more commonly used symbols in the resources section at the back of this book (see Appendix 4). An excellent way of encouraging your students to use and understand these symbols is to photocopy them to go in the front of student exercise books, going through their meanings with your class. Even the youngest children should be able to understand and use these symbols.

Different ways of marking

'Marking' comes in many different forms: from the helpful to the destructive, from the detailed to the generalized. I am well aware of how time-consuming detailed marking can be, and how complex the subject is as a whole. In fact, I devoted a long section to this area of the teacher's job in my book for NQTs, *Starting Teaching: How to Succeed and Survive*.* At the heart of marking is the need for a balancing act – we just cannot, as working teachers, mark every single piece of work in full detail. Consequently, we need to make decisions about how we are going to mark each piece of writing, and consider different strategies that we might use to make the job more effective and less time-intensive. Below are some thoughts on the different ways of marking that we might employ, and in the following section some strategies for getting the marking done.

---

*Sue Cowley, *Starting Teaching: How to Succeed and Survive* (London: Continuum, 2001).

- *Close marking*: Many people (including parents, managers and inspectors) might view this as the 'ideal' form of marking. With this style of marking, each and every error is identified, and detailed comments are made on how the student can improve their work. Close marking does have its drawbacks: firstly, it is extremely time-consuming for the teacher, and secondly, it can be offputting (and sometimes damaging) for students to receive back their writing, completely covered in the teacher's pen. However, close marking can be very successful in helping older and very able students to develop complex pieces of writing such as essays.
- *Tick and flick*: This type of marking involves placing a big tick or cross at the end of each paragraph or page, then turning (or 'flicking') to the next. This exercise might be followed by a brief comment at the end of the piece of writing. Although we might be able to say that we have 'marked' the children's work, this method is not particularly effective when it comes to the students actually learning from their mistakes. However, children do like to have their work 'marked', to see a series of ticks on their work. In addition, the teacher will gain a sense of how well the children are doing and what areas need further work.
- *Marking for specific errors or features*: With this type of marking, the teacher identifies an area of concern, or a feature on which they would like the students to concentrate before the writing takes place. For instance, the children might be asked to focus particularly on getting their punctuation right, or to think carefully about how they paragraph their work. These specific aspects are then looked at closely by the teacher as he or she marks the work.

Of course, the majority of us employ marking strategies that fall somewhere in the middle of all the above, depending on the amount of time that we can afford to give to marking the work. It is useful sometimes to step back and consider how the marking that you do actually impacts on the quality of your children's learning. Although 'ticking and flicking' might make their books 'look' marked, how much good is this form of marking actually doing? If you tend to focus more on 'close' marking, consider whether your students might feel that this implies a criticism of their writing, and whether it is actually demotivating for them.

Strategies for marking

It is tempting to view marking as something that the teacher does for the children. However, this need not always be the case. In fact, some of the best learning can come from employing different, more unusual, strategies. Here are just a few ideas for you to try, which will also save some of your valuable time.

- *Marking each other's work*: Asking your children to swap over their writing, and to make evaluative comments on their classmates' work, can be a very effective marking strategy. The children really enjoy the chance to 'play teacher'. This strategy can help motivate your students, as it shows them just what others within their peer group are achieving. In addition, looking at other people's work (whether 'good' or 'bad') will help them consider what is, or is not, effective writing.
- *Marking the work together*: There are many opportunities for written work to be marked as a whole-class activity, especially where the writing has a factual basis, for instance with spelling or maths tests. The teacher gives a series of answers, and the students tick or cross their own answers and give themselves a mark or grade. The students could either mark their own work (if you trust them!) or they could swap over and mark somebody else's.
- *Marking across peer groups*: An interesting alternative, especially for the secondary teacher with several teaching groups, is to ask your older students to mark the work of their younger counterparts, and vice versa. As well as playing the role of 'experts', this is also useful where you have a class underachieving (for instance, in Year 9) and another group with high levels of achievement (for example, in Year 7). The embarrassment of marking work that is actually better than theirs, although done by younger students, should make them buck up their ideas.

Approaching exams

As exam time approaches, students can start to experience high levels of stress. This time will probably be especially difficult for your weakest students, who may be used to 'failing'. It could also be that some of your more able students do not perform to the best of their ability when under the pressure of time. There are various ways in which we as teachers can help our students approach exams.

- *Give them plenty of practice*: The more exam practice students have, the more comfortable they will feel with the idea of the approaching exam. See the following section for more thoughts on why this is so important.
- *Teach them how to revise*: If revision is needed for the exam, spend time helping your students find strategies for doing it. They might need to be taught techniques for memorizing facts, or effective ways of approaching revision.
- *Boost their self-esteem*: Make it clear to your weakest or most nervous students that exams are not the 'be all and end all' in life. Although GCSEs and A levels are clearly very important for their future, you as a teacher can still value them as individuals, whatever grades they achieve in their exams. If your students are taking their SATs exams, let them know that as well as their externally assessed exam grades you are also able to give them a grade based on your own assessment of their work in the classroom.
- *Take advantage of their increased motivation*: As exam time approaches, students generally become much more motivated. They realize that it is important for them to do well, and will tend to work harder in class. Take advantage of this increase in motivation, perhaps by working on important coursework, or by getting them to write high-quality pieces for teacher assessment.

Preparing for exams

There is a great deal that we can do to prepare our students for their written exams, both by giving them information about what the exam will involve, and also by letting them know how to go about getting the best results that they can. Again, there is no 'secret' to doing well in exams – simply a range of strategies and approaches that can be learned. Don't forget that for children with particular special needs, additional help or time may be allowed in the exams. Do check with your examinations officer in advance to see if this applies to any of your students. Here are some ideas about how you might prepare your own students for their exams, at whatever age.

- *Practice, practice, practice*: If you are teaching an 'examination year', exam practice should become a regular part of your classroom routine. There are a number of good reasons for this. With regular practice your students will realize that there is nothing (or little) to be scared of. They will get used to the general format of the exam paper and start to understand what the examiners are asking them to do. They will learn about timing, and how to allocate the correct amount of time to each piece of writing. They can also be educated in the way that exams run – in the importance of working in complete silence, and not glancing across at what their friends are doing. Finally, although exam practice can add to your marking load, you will at least get a number of 'lessons off' from teacher-led work.
- *Plan, plan, plan*: There is no need to always write out a full exam answer when you are doing exam practice. A good-quality plan will show you whether or not the student understands how to answer the question. Planning in class also helps your students understand the importance of this part of the writing process, and to practise the skills involved.
- *Information is power (1)*: Do get your hands on some old exam papers, but don't keep them to yourself. Please share them with your students! There is nothing more frightening than the unknown, and facing an exam paper never having seen a similar one before will be highly confusing for your children. They may well waste a great deal of time trying to understand exactly what the exam paper is asking them to do – time that would be better spent proving their abilities.
- *Information is power (2)*: As well as sharing exam papers with

your students, don't be afraid to show them the marking criteria. If they wish to gain maximum marks, they need to fulfil these criteria, and it is therefore essential that your students understand what they must aim to achieve. For instance, how vital is good technique – accurate spelling, punctuation, etc.? Do they need to show an understanding of metaphor and simile within their analysis?

- *Show them sample essays*: A good way of demonstrating how they might earn the best marks possible is to show your students a sample essay or exam answer. This might be from a high-quality answer from a previous year's exam, or it could be an essay that you write yourself to demonstrate how the question is best answered. If you show them a student's work, why not ask them to give a mark according to how well they think that student would have done?

- *Work on sample answers as a whole class*: A good way of approaching exam practice is to split your class into groups, and ask them to formulate an answer together, before sharing their ideas with the class. This takes away the pressure of individual work, and also allows all the students to contribute their ideas to the class as a whole.

- *Show the connection between questions and marks*: Some students 'freeze up' in exams, and fail to look at what the paper tells them about the amount of marks available for each question. Teach your children that there is no point in writing copious amounts for a question that will only ever earn them two or three marks. Similarly, make sure they realize that some questions are well worth answering in detail, because they offer the chance to earn a high number of marks. Often, if a question has a number of marks available, the students will be given one mark for every separate point they make on the subject. Do share this information with them.

- *Show the importance of timing*: Succeeding in exams has a lot to do with the ability to time your writing, to avoid getting so carried away that you use up all your time on one question out of two, thereby cutting your potential marks in half. Again, practice under exam conditions will help your students learn how to time themselves. If the exam involves writing long essays, it is a good idea for them to write the time that they should finish on their answer booklet, and if they run over, to start the next essay while leaving time and space to finish the first one, should they have some spare time at the end of the exam.

- *Show the importance of the question's phrasing*: Exam questions tend to be phrased in a particular way, one that encourages the student to give the correct answer, in the correct form, and referring to the appropriate material. As you spend time going through old papers or questions, take time to look at the language of the questions. Here are just some of the things that you might consider about the way in which a question is phrased.
  - Is the question in two or more parts? If it is, do the different parts earn you equal marks, or is one part more important than another? Some exam questions may look as though they only have one part, for instance when they are written in a single paragraph, but are actually asking two separate questions.
  - Does the question say something like 'According to the passage what does ...?' This means that the students must make close reference to the passage in their answer, or use relevant quotations.
  - Does the question ask you to use a specific form or layout in your answer? If it does, ensure you use the tone that is relevant to that particular form.
  - Is there a particular viewpoint that is best for answering this question?
  - How much detail do you need to give to receive the maximum amount of marks?

Answering exam questions

As well as preparing your students for their exams, you can also help them with the actual writing of their answers. Again, it is well worth spending some class time going over the techniques with them. For many, these strategies are not immediately obvious, and they do need to be taught what they are and how to use them. Here are some ideas you might like to share with your class or classes.

- *Choosing the question*: If there is a choice of questions on the paper, talk with your students about how they might choose the best one to answer. You might discuss how their individual strengths could lead them to answer one question better than another.

- *Sticking to the question*: You can find more ideas about this in Chapter 4 ('Answering the question', p. 71). Do assure your children that there is no need to write down everything they know on a subject. If the material they include does not answer the question, they will earn no marks for it.

- *Use the question to start your answer*: Again, this idea is explained in detail in Chapter 4 (p. 72). For many children, it is getting started in an exam that causes them problems. The idea of this technique is to use the actual wording of the question to begin your answer, because this helps you get started and to stay 'on track'.

- *Keep it simple*: Sometimes more able children will start to over-complicate things in exams, to assume that the answers must be more difficult than they appear to be. Encourage your students to take a step back from the paper, consider carefully what they are being asked, and then word their answer in as straightforward a way as possible.

- *Don't waffle*: Similarly, some children feel the need to write at great length, when a brief, concise answer would in fact be better. This can cause problems with running out of time, and can also lose them marks if the examiner feels that they haven't stuck to the question. Encourage students who have a tendency to waffle to look closely at the marks available for each answer and to write only what is needed to earn those marks.

8 The writing clinic

This chapter provides a brief 'writing clinic', in which some of the most common writing problems are explored, using a series of case-studies. For each case-study, I provide an example of the problem, a 'diagnosis' of why the specific problem is occurring, and strategies for the teacher to use in overcoming the child's particular area of weakness. I have included writing from a range of different ages, to illustrate the problems at different stages in a child's school career, and also to help you consider the next stage of development in the child's written work. You will find many of these problems cropping up in various degrees of seriousness throughout a child's career at school.

Overwriting

The ripe orange sun bled into the dark blue sea, like a huge orange being squeezed of its juice. A soft, gentle breeze caressed the pure white sand of the beach. The pretty young girl swept her long curling blonde hair back from her face and sighed deeply, a sad, mournful look on her pale, smooth-skinned face.

'O John. How beautiful it is here. What a wonderful day I've had with you. I'm so sad that it has to end.'

Diagnosis
This piece of writing has everything but the kitchen sink! It is melodramatic rather than realistic, in fact it sounds like something from a trashy romance novel. The writer loves using description and descriptive words, particularly adjectives, and

the way that she can make them sound. She may have recently learned about similes and other language devices, and be trying to experiment with them (although not very successfully). She enjoys writing, but has little sense of how the writing might appear to the reader.

Strategies

- *Get an overview*: Ask the student to step back from the work and look at its overall effect. Reading it out loud, perhaps to another student, might help.
- *Find a tone*: Ask the student to try reading the piece in a variety of different tones, from the 'plain', to the 'pacy', to the 'melodramatic', to see which one fits best to what she has written. This should give her a sense of how over-written the work actually is.
- *Talk about adjectives*: Identify what an adjective is, if the student does not already know. Now ask her to rewrite the piece, removing all the adjectives, and finding other ways of putting across any description that is required.

Dull or under-writing

> The boy went into the room. There was a table and four chairs in the room. He went over to the chairs and sat down. While he waited for the man to arrive he looked around the room. Then he looked at his watch and wondered when the man would come.

Diagnosis

This piece is 'under-written' because of the total lack of description and limited vocabulary. It is also dull, because nothing of any interest happens.

Strategies

- *Consider the choice of verbs*: Ask the student to look at the verbs he has chosen, for instance 'went', and to try to find a more interesting alternative that suggests something about the boy's character. For instance, he might 'stride' or 'storm' into the room.

- *Consider the use of descriptive language*: Although you want to avoid an overly descriptive, adjective-laden style, the reader needs some type of detail to be able to visualize what is happening. For instance, when the boy looks around the room, what does he see?
- *Consider the development of character*: Using more interesting verbs, and adding some description, will give a stronger sense of character. Ask the student to empathize with the character – what is he thinking and feeling, and how might this be shown in the way that he moves or reacts to his situation?

Stilted writing

Jane was five. It was her birthday. For her birthday she got a toy. The toy was nice. It was a doll. She played with the doll. She had a party. She had fun.

Diagnosis

This piece is typical of the early, or emerging, writer. It has a stilted style and does not yet flow sufficiently well, making the reader feel that it is very disjointed and 'choppy'. The child does not yet have a sufficiently wide vocabulary to avoid the standard single-clause 'subject–verb–object'-type sentences. She needs to find some way of joining up the sentences.

Strategies

- *Use of connectives*: The child needs to develop her 'bank' of connecting words, so that the short sentences can be joined together. The teacher could give her a list of connecting words to try out on this piece of writing, for instance 'and', 'but', 'then', etc.
- *Use of description*: As in the example above of 'dull' writing, the child is not giving the reader any sense of what the people and objects are like. One way of helping her might be

to ask her to describe the doll on its own – what does it look like, what colour is it, what clothes does it wear? This description could then be added into the piece.

- *Developing character*: Again, the writer needs to think about her character, and the way that she is feeling. So far, we only know that Jane had 'fun'. Talk to the child about how her character felt at the birthday party. What did she eat? Did she have a cake and did she like it?

Lack of punctuation

Sammy raced out of the door and ran down the street he was late for school and he knew that he would get in trouble when he got to school. when he got to school he sped into the classroom but the teacher had already taken the register and Sammy got into trouble again he hated getting into trouble. why are you late again Sammy the teacher asked I woke up late Sammy said because my alarm didnt go off then you need to mend your alarm the teacher told Sammy. youre in detention with me after school now get on with your work

Diagnosis
This child's writing has a strong sense of pace, but an almost complete lack of punctuation. In a rush to get the ideas down, he has become wrapped up in telling the story rather than thinking about the needs of the reader.

Strategies
- *Reading back*: Ask the child to read his own work back to you. This will help him to see that the reader needs punctuation to show where there is a pause. Tell the student to pause every time he would naturally take a breath in his reading, and this will help to indicate where the full stops or commas should go.
- *Forming the sentences*: With a writer whose punctuation is weak, a good tip is to ask him to form each sentence in his

head before it is written down. He can then work on one
sentence at a time, adding full stops where necessary.

- *Punctuating dialogue*: The writer has also neglected to
  punctuate the speech. Ask him to underline or highlight
  the words in the passage that are actually spoken, to help
  him punctuate the dialogue.

Repetitive writing

Jamie climbed up into the cave. Then he took his torch out.
Then he shone his torch around the cave. The cave was dark
and Jamie couldn't see what was at the back. Then he
walked to the back of the cave. When he got to the back of
the cave he shone his torch again. When he did this he saw a
big spider. When he saw the spider he got very scared. Then
he ran out of the cave.

Diagnosis
This writing is very repetitive, and consequently sounds stilted. It
is also dull for the reader, because of the lack of variation in the
vocabulary. There is excessive use of the word 'then' – a fairly
common problem for younger writers who are trying to divide
their work up into sentences, and show the chain of events
chronologically, but who are not yet using a sufficient variety of
adverbs to show the time sequence.

Strategies
- *Identify the repetition*: Ask the child to underline any word that
  is repeated more than twice in the piece of writing. In this
  case, the words 'cave', 'then' and 'when'.
- *Look for alternatives*: Talk to the child about how a noun such
  as cave might be replaced by the word 'it'. Alternatively, it is
  often possible to remove the noun altogether, for instance in
  the sentence 'Then he shone his torch around the cave.', the
  words 'the cave' could be completely removed. The
  sentence would still make sense, as the reader already knows
  where Jamie is.

- *Develop a bank of adverbs*: The writer needs to find alternatives to the chain of 'thens' and 'whens'. At this stage, a bank of words which show a sequence of events would be useful: 'first', 'next', 'finally', and so on.

Part 4

Writing: Around the Subject

9 Writing for all

The aim for us as teachers is to get *all* our students to learn to write, and preferably to learn to write well. If they don't succeed in this challenge, they will be handicapped for the rest of their lives. Those who are not fully literate are restricted in the type of employment that they can find when they leave school. They are also limited in their ability to communicate via the written word, whether it is in a letter, an email, a job application, and so on. We owe it to all our children to develop their writing to the best of our (and their) ability, and this chapter is about how we might achieve this: for the least able and the gifted, the boys as well as the girls, those for whom English is a second language and those who find it difficult to behave themselves.

Helping the least able

I can imagine that it must be hugely frustrating for those children who find writing a real challenge. Day after day they arrive at school, knowing all too well that they are going to have to write in the vast majority of their lessons. It is hardly surprising that some of these children only seem to enjoy the practical subjects, such as PE, drama and art. At least in these areas they can communicate their ideas and complete the activities without the challenge that writing means for them. It also does not surprise me that these students will often lose their focus during lesson time and resort to bad behaviour. This may be as a result of their embarrassment when they find a relatively simple task so challenging. In order to hide their discomfort, they play the 'class clown' or give the teacher a hard time.

How, then, can we assist our least able students, and also those who have specific special needs? How can we help them, not only in improving their writing, but also in staying motivated to continue the struggle, without resorting to poor behaviour? Here are a few ideas for you to try out with those children in your classes who find writing as challenging as scaling Mount Everest.

- *Don't believe the worst*: It is very tempting for us as teachers to judge our least able students. The frustration of being presented with poor pieces of writing time after time can make us believe that these students are simply not making any effort. While this might be true for a small minority, do try to assume that your children have tried their hardest, whilst still insisting that they strive to achieve better results next time. In addition, ensure that you check whether the children who present you with poor writing on a regular basis have been identified as having a special need. If not, make sure they are assessed by a special needs teacher.
- *Stay positive*: Similarly, it is very tempting to become negative when presented with what you might consider to be 'rubbish'. Whilst I am not suggesting that you should praise poor work, try to be aware that these children will be faced with negativity and failure day after day, and that this cycle needs to be broken. Try to retain a positive approach, looking for what *has* worked in their writing rather than focusing on what hasn't. It could be that their ideas are in fact excellent, and it is merely the technique that prevents you from appreciating this.
- *Watch your language*: As part of this struggle to remain positive, take care over what you say to your least able children. When you are tired or stressed, it is all too easy to throw off a casual comment, such as 'this is terrible – you haven't made much effort with it, have you?' Whilst this might relieve the stress for us as teachers, do bear in mind that the child could take this type of comment very personally indeed. Writing is very personal – what we put down on the page is an expression of ourselves. It is hard for any writer, no matter what age they are, to accept criticism of their work. Instead, try to phrase your constructive criticisms in a positive way, perhaps identifying one thing

that the child has done well (even if this is as simple as putting a title on their work).

- *Set them targets*: Everyone needs something to strive for, but for the weak writer it may feel as though there is so much that needs putting right, there is no point in even trying. As teachers, we can assist our children in developing their writing by setting them small, achievable targets, and ensuring that we reward them when they achieve each one. For instance, you might ask a child to aim for the neatest handwriting that they can produce, and reward good effort with a sticker.

- *Give them a break*: Sometimes, it is worth giving the weakest writers a break from writing, especially those for whom the technical demands of their work prove very stressful. On occasions, why not offer them the opportunity to use a 'scribe'? This could be the class teacher, a learning assistant, or even another child. Using a scribe allows the least able to focus on the content of their work, rather than worrying about technique. Alternatively, you could ask them to use a tape to record their work, challenging them to develop their oral as well as their written skills. Again, this would allow them to focus on developing the content of their work, without worrying about the need to spell, write neatly, and so on. They could follow up this taping of their work by writing one part of it down, as neatly and accurately as possible.

- *Use group activities*: For the least able, working as part of a group can prove a welcome relief from the stress of individual writing. In a mixed-ability setting, the more able children will often help their less able counterparts to succeed. In addition, the least able can choose to complete those tasks that are best suited to their own talents, for instance drawing work. For more ideas, look at the group projects described in Chapter 6 (pp. 129–31).

Extending the gifted writer

At the opposite end of the spectrum from our least able students are the gifted and very able writers. It is difficult for a teacher in a mixed-ability classroom to offer challenges to those at the top end of the ability range, while still giving the opportunity for the middle- and low-ability children to succeed. The ideas below give you some thoughts about developing and extending the written work of the most able in your class. You can find some additional comments in Chapter 4 ('Essay-writing with the most able', pp. 82–3).

- *Work on their 'voice'*: One of the hardest things for a writer is to find their own tone, their personal writing style or 'voice'. Encourage your able students to hear their own voice internally as they work, listening to the sound of the writing in their heads. Developing a 'voice' might mean adding splashes of humour to the work, or adapting the way in which they use punctuation and italics to give emphasis. It could be applying a more informal voice to what is traditionally approached as a formal subject. A good way of developing your own voice as a writer is to practise 'echoing' the voice that other writers use, for instance writing a detective story 'in the style of' Elmore Leonard or Raymond Chandler.
- *Use rewriting activities*: A useful exercise for very able students is to ask them to rewrite the work of other authors, but in a different style. For instance, you might ask them to rewrite a broadsheet newspaper article in the style of a tabloid; you could get them to turn an adult story into a children's one; or perhaps to change a formal letter into an informal one, adapting the vocabulary and style as appropriate. Rewriting other texts in this active way will help them learn about all the different aspects that go to make up a good piece of writing.
- *Use analysis activities*: For the very able, a good way of developing their knowledge about writing and language is to ask them to analyse the way that other writers work. This knowledge can then be adapted and applied to their own writing. For instance, they might look at how writers in different genres structure their sentences to create a sense of pace and rhythm, and to develop tension. They could look for the use of language devices within a text (see below) and

consider the effects that these create. The best writers are often the most avid readers, and they are no doubt already subconsciously analysing the books that they read.

- *Develop linguistic techniques*: Able students should be capable, from a very young age, of developing imagery and other linguistic techniques in their work. Don't be afraid to introduce these techniques early on, either on an individual or a whole-class basis. In my experience (and as I have already noted) children love encountering new, technical terms such as metaphor, alliteration and pathetic fallacy. For instance, your students might use repetition to emphasize a point; they could use an extended metaphor to give their work a sense of style; they might use alliteration to create a more interesting sound for the reader. These techniques can be used right across the curriculum, rather than simply in work done in English lessons.

- *Develop the use of punctuation*: Encourage your very able students to explore a more advanced use of punctuation. For instance, teach them when it is appropriate to use a colon or semicolon, and the syntactical rules behind this.

- *Break the rules*: Students who are very able in the technique of writing may need to learn how to bend the rules once in a while. The 'best' writers are not merely technically accurate but also need imagination and the willingness to experiment. The more conscious this bending of the rules is, the better it will work. Rather than simply making mistakes, bending the rules shows that a writer has complete control of their writing style. For instance, they might play with grammar to create a sense of personal style, perhaps splitting the odd infinitive when they feel it is appropriate. Another example might be a writer who uses the conjunctions 'and' or 'but' to start a sentence, in order to create a better sound, flow or pace in their writing.

- *Develop vocabulary*: Do ensure that the most able writers have access to a thesaurus, whether on paper or on the computer. This will help them to develop a wider vocabulary, and to consider a range of words, picking out the one that is most appropriate to the context and sound of what they are writing. Encourage them to explore the definition of unfamiliar words, using a dictionary to consider the subtle variations of meaning that are available.

- *Think about sound*: The best writers consider the sound of the words that they use, as well as their meaning. We tend to associate word sounds with writing poetry, but in fact this applies in any form of writing, and across the whole curriculum. Again, encourage them to consider the way that their language would sound when read out loud by 'hearing' their writing in their heads. Also, ask them to think about how words with different sounds might add interest to their work.

- *Encourage a sense of self*: As well as their own 'voice', good writers put a sense of themselves into their work. This might mean offering an emotional response to the subject, as described in Chapter 4 ('Introductions and conclusions', p. 80). It might mean referring to personal experiences to back up the comments that they make on a subject.

- *Encourage intertextual reference*: Higher up the school, able students should be encouraged to look for texts which they can make reference to in their writing. Intertextual reference might involve quoting an acknowledged expert on a subject, or it could mean referring to a link that they have discovered between one novel or author and another.

Boys and writing

There has been much debate and discussion about why it is that boys are less successful in their writing than girls. I would argue that an important part of the problem is our own perceptions as teachers of the ways in which boys write, as well as the actual quality of their work. This, however, is a book of ideas and strategies and consequently not the place for a debate of this nature. Rather, I would like to offer some practical tips that have worked for me in the classroom when teaching boys how to develop their writing. I would like to apologize in advance for what some might see as the stereotyped and generalized nature of some of what follows. (In my defence I should emphasize that these ideas all arise from my own classroom experience.) In addition, many of these tips will work as well with girls as they do with boys. My main goal is simply to offer you strategies that will work, rather than to be politically correct!

- *Consider quality v. quantity*: Some boys turn out shorter pieces of writing than their female classmates, and the natural tendency is for us to make a judgement based on quantity as well as quality. However, the best and most effective pieces of writing are often concise. When marking and assessing work, try to consider whether the boys in your class achieve as much as the girls, by simply using less words.
- *Be gender-neutral*: The majority of primary school teachers are female, and being a woman surely affects our perceptions of our students' work. It is probably fair to say that men and women have different priorities in their reading interests, and in what they view as 'good' writing. It is of course hard for a female teacher to judge a male student's writing from a neutral perspective. However, when you read and mark your students' work do try hard to judge it from a 'gender-neutral' position. For instance, I was once presented with a hard-hitting action story as a piece of coursework. From my own, female, perspective, I did not feel particularly inclined to award a high mark to this story, even though I enjoy reading thrillers outside the classroom. However, when I stood back from my own perceptions and looked at the quality of the writing itself, I could see that it was in fact a good piece of work.
- *Find out what inspires them*: Certain genres can be very appealing to boys, for instance science fiction, fantasy and horror. Find out which areas of fiction appeal to the boys that you teach and capitalize on their interests. Try to encourage them to read within these genres as well, as this will inevitably have a positive impact on their writing. If you do have reluctant older readers in your class, why not offer them a book of short stories to start with. Alternatively, even reading comics or magazines is better than nothing.
- *Use the media*: In my experience, media-based writing is very popular with boys (and with girls for that matter). If we need or want to develop our students' motivation to write, we should try to incorporate this type of media work into at

least some of our lessons. For instance, reading magazines is a popular activity with boys, and as teachers we can utilize this interest to engage them. You can find some ideas about a group media project on magazines in Chapter 6 (p. 130). In addition, writing a script that will eventually be videoed can also lead to high levels of enthusiasm.

- *Use group projects*: Again, my classroom experience suggests that boys produce good work when they are given a group project, especially one that covers a topic of interest to them (football, computer games and wrestling spring to mind). The talents of our students lie in many different areas of the wide field of 'writing', and a group project allows each person to bring their particular abilities to the task.

- *Use computer games*: I am not suggesting that you should encourage your students to play computer games in the classroom. However, many computer games do actually contain a very strong (and sequenced) narrative that might be useful in encouraging your students to write stories. Talk to your students about the games that they play on their computers, and analyse the way that the narratives are structured within them.

- *Use visualization*: Another tip is to ask your students to visualize each part of a story, either viewing it as a movie in their heads, or drawing up a storyboard of the sequence of events that take place. The ability to see the sequence of events in our heads plays an important part in good story-writing.

- *Action v. description*: I would argue that, on the whole, boys enjoy and succeed in writing action-based pieces, while girls tend more towards the descriptive. When setting a subject for class writing, why not offer a few different topics, some which lend themselves to descriptive writing and others which lean more towards action.

- *'Slugs and snails!!!'*: Being asked to write about something disgusting will motivate many of our students, whether they are boys or girls. This might be writing about a repulsive alien who comes to Earth, it could be drawing and labelling a design of the most hideous-looking monster in the Universe, it might be writing a recipe for the most disgusting cake ever made.

Teaching students with ESL/EAL

Teaching students whose first language is not English can be very rewarding. Not only are they generally keen to learn and to work, but they also bring with them to the classroom a huge range of cultural and life experiences that differ from the 'norm'. The majority of us have only ever learned a second language at school, and then only for a relatively short space of time. However, these bi- or trilingual children have the advantage of being completely immersed in the English language, at least during the course of the school day. Although we may feel that they are slow to pick up the words at first, eventually this immersion will lead to a far greater and deeper knowledge of their new language. Here are some tips and thoughts about working with children who have English as a second or additional language. Many of these ideas are taken from my experience of working in a multilingual international school.

- *Grammatical understanding*: The difference between the structure of the mother tongue and of the English language will often result in grammatical errors, for instance in the placement of verbs within a sentence. It is well worth spending time teaching a child with ESL about word order and other areas of English grammar. This can be done even with the child who has only a limited vocabulary.
- *Grammatical awareness*: You can help both the child and your class as a whole by developing their grammatical awareness. For instance, you might look at the way in which regular verbs are conjugated in English. This would be useful not only for the child learning the language, but also for the other students in your class, as it will make them more aware of the way that their own language works.
- *Irregular verbs*: These can be very confusing for ESL children, and it is a good idea to give them lists of how to conjugate the most commonly used irregular verbs, such as 'to be'.
- *A two-way learning process*: Why not widen your knowledge by asking the ESL children to teach you some words in their language? This can provide a wonderful opportunity for us to pick up the basics of a second language, sometimes a very

unusual language that we might normally never have the chance to hear. It also offers a wonderful way of motivating the children and making them feel included in the classroom.

- *Make them an expert*: In addition, why not ask the children (as long as they are confident enough) to share a few words of their language with the class. They might teach the numbers from one to ten, the days of the week, or different parts of the body. You may be surprised how receptive children are to learning another language (especially the younger ones), and you can have some great fun at the same time. Being an 'expert' in this way allows the children with ESL to feel that they too have an important contribution to make to the class.
- *Give them key vocabulary*: It is well worth giving ESL children a list of key terms or technical words in all the subjects of the curriculum. In fact, depending on the age of your children, you could give lists of these subject-specific words (mainly nouns) to the whole class. The children who already speak English could learn them as spellings, while the ESL students could learn them as new vocabulary. To take this one stage further, an ESL child could play 'teacher' and read out the spellings for the rest of the class during a spelling test.
- *Give them a translator*: If you have two children in your class who have the same mother tongue, but who are at different stages in their acquisition of English, why not ask one of them to act as a translator for the other?
- *Be aware of cultural differences*: Language divides us because we cannot understand each other, but it also divides us at a cultural level. Try to be aware of, or learn about, the culture from which your ESL students come, and how this might affect them within the classroom. For instance, the use of irony is prevalent in the English language, but many other cultures find it hard to understand, and consequently do not 'get' our humour. To give another example, some languages are written in a way that we would consider to be 'back to front', i.e. from right to left on the page, and from the back of a book to the front.
- *Work with texts from other countries*: Try to incorporate some

texts from other countries and cultures into your classroom, whether in the original language or in translation (or even both). This sort of activity could provide you with some excellent written work with a multicultural basis.

- *Penpals*: To develop this work further, why not find overseas penpals for all your students? There are some useful penpal websites listed in Appendix 2 at the back of this book.
- *Find out about other countries*: In addition, why not use a project on the child's homeland as part of your class work? This could be especially effective in the primary school, or in the geography class. You might ask the child to be an 'expert', talking to the class about what their country of origin is like, although do consult with them first, to check that they are happy to do this.

Writing and behaviour

For some children, writing is difficult or impossible because they simply cannot behave themselves. This might be because of a lack of concentration or because they get involved in low-level misbehaviour, such as chatting and getting out of their seats. If this is the case with one or more of your students, your first priority must be to ensure good behaviour from all of your class. In my book *Getting the Buggers to Behave* you can find a wide range of practical ideas for improving behaviour in your classroom. Here are just a few tips that will help ensure that your children behave properly, so that they can write to the best of their ability.

- *Set your boundaries*: As we saw in Chapter 1, the successful teacher sets boundaries for how written work will take place. If your boundaries are made sufficiently explicit from the start, your students will soon learn that this is the way they are expected to work. Your boundaries should be both for behaviour, and also for the quality and quantity of work that you expect to receive.
- *Explain your aims*: By setting out the aims of the lesson clearly for your students, you will 'signpost' the learning that is going to take place. To understand the importance of aims, think about how you might plan a piece of work

before you begin to write. For instance, you might write out a list of points you are going to include, and put these in the correct order before you start. In the same way that you need these 'signposts' to tell you where the writing is going, your students will benefit greatly from signposts about what they are going to learn during a lesson.

- *Always be polite*: Being polite is not only about the way you interact with your children, but also about the way that you react to their work. Whilst it can be tempting to 'slag off' a piece of writing that you feel is of poor quality, this can be extremely destructive and demotivating to a child, especially to a child who finds writing difficult. In addition, you may well encourage poor behaviour if a child feels their work is not valued. If you believe that a poor piece of work is a result of laziness, rather than weakness, you can still react politely. For instance, you might say 'I just know you can do much better than this' rather than 'This is an awful piece of writing.'

- *Stay positive*: This idea has been mentioned earlier in this chapter. However, I am happy to repeat myself because I view it as a vital strategy for motivating your students. If you can react in a positive way to a poor piece of writing, rather than in a negative or critical way, you will encourage your students to continue improving their work. For instance, set targets about specific aspects of the writing that need improvement, saying 'I want you to focus on putting the punctuation in the correct place' rather than 'your use of punctuation is terrible.'

- *Set individual targets*: To develop this idea further, targets can be extremely useful for individual students who find writing difficult. Be careful that the targets you set are realistic, and think about exactly how many targets to set at one time. It is better to set a single specific target, such as 'put a full stop at the end of every sentence', rather than a generalized target or set of targets such as 'get your punctuation and spelling right'.

- *Set whole-class targets*: In *Getting the Buggers to Behave*, I explained a very successful idea for setting whole-class targets that another teacher had shared with me. With this technique, the teacher divides the work up for the class by saying: 'this is the work you *must* do, this is the work you *should* do, and this is the work you *could* do'. By dividing the work into these three categories, the teacher sets clear boundaries for what must be completed. In addition, the more able students will be stretched, while the less able will retain a sense of achievement.

- *Use repetition*: How many times have you been faced by the situation where you explain a task and then find, a few minutes later, that several hands go up from students saying 'I don't understand what we're meant to do'? In the same way that you might repeat the name of a student who is misbehaving before you sanction them, you can use repetition when setting a piece of written work. After explaining the task, ask one of your students to repeat back to you the work that has been set. In this way you can clarify any misunderstandings at an early stage.

- *Know when to be flexible*: At certain times of the day or week, or under certain conditions that are out of your control, your students' written work may not be as good as you wish. For instance, a class returning from a lively PE lesson may find it very hard to settle down to written work, and it may be better to do some spoken activities with them instead. Similarly, on a wet Friday afternoon, your students might achieve little of real value if they are asked to do an extended piece of writing. Know when to be flexible, and when practical work, speaking tasks or reading might be more appropriate than writing. Better to be realistic than to struggle with your children, forcing them to write, creating a sense of resentment and achieving little of real value.

- *Teaching styles*: For those students with poor concentration, or in a class where there is quite a lot of bad behaviour, we need to think carefully about suiting our teaching styles to the children that we teach. The National Literacy Strategy encourages us to begin our lessons with a fast-paced 'starter activity', and this is one good way of encouraging students with a lack of focus to get into the mood for writing. Starting each lesson in a similar manner helps to give a sense of structure to the work. However, teaching from the front is not necessarily the best teaching style for an entire lesson, especially where the class tends to drift off-task easily. A good teaching style for poorly behaved children is one that sets shorter targets, and rewards the completion of each part of the work. Although this style may take up more of the teacher's energy, the reward of better behaviour will lead to a more positive atmosphere in the classroom.

- *Developing focus*: To write well, we need to be able to focus on the task in hand. If your students have poor concentration, and cannot stick at a written task for a long period of time, consider using some of the focus exercises described in Chapter 1 (pp. 14–15). As I suggested above, you should also aim to offer short, targeted activities, as these will give the students a stronger sense of focus and achievement.

10 Writing and ICT

For some people, writing on a computer seems almost like cheating. There is a feeling that computers make the writer lazy, that they do the work for us, checking our spelling and grammar or offering us an electronic thesaurus when we can't find the right word. I would never suggest that computers could or should replace the need for our children to learn how to spell. Nor should they take away the necessity for learning what is and isn't grammatically correct, or how to use a dictionary or a thesaurus. However, we should embrace the advantages that using ICT can bring, whilst bearing in mind its disadvantages.

This chapter looks at the ways in which ICT can be used to motivate and develop your children's writing. It explores the advantages and disadvantages of using computers as a teaching tool, and it also looks at resources such as the internet and email. As a writer and teacher, I make daily use of ICT, both inside and outside the classroom. My books are produced on a computer from the very first words to the final layout and submission. I also do much of my research on the internet, and I am in daily contact with other teachers and writers via email. As I said in the introduction to this book, the increasing use of technology means that writing becomes ever *more* important, not less. After all, the internet allows adults and children from all over the world to publish their ideas and their writing in a public forum where anyone can access it.

When you are using ICT in the classroom, do bear in mind that your students (however young they are) may well know more about computers than you do. Today's children have grown up with this technology, whereas many teachers would not have even been taught to use the most basic computers when they were at school. So, do make sure that you utilize the knowledge that your students have, and if there are experts on different aspects of ICT in your classroom, get them to help teach both you and the rest of your class.

Writing on a computer

Advantages
The secret of effective ICT use in the classroom is to consider the advantages that it brings and to maximize these for our students. It is tempting just to see the word processor as a presentational tool, especially if you are not particularly computer-literate. However, its uses go way beyond simply producing 'pretty' pieces of work. Here are some ideas about the advantages that writing on a computer can bring.

- *A building tool*: Word-processing software allows the writer a wonderful degree of flexibility. You can build a basic outline of a piece first, then fill in the gaps bit by bit, elaborating on each idea in turn. This initial outline can act as a useful plan, indicating the order in which the ideas will come, where the paragraph breaks should be, and so on. (See the section in Chapter 6, pp. 121–23, entitled 'Building your writing' for some ideas about this approach. In addition, see the section below entitled 'The computer as a writing tool', p. 184, for a more detailed explanation of how you can use computers to help your children develop their written work.)
- *An editing tool*: Word processors also allow us to edit our work with remarkable ease. We can cut out whole sections, move a paragraph from the beginning to the end of a piece of writing, change single words, alter sentence structure, and so on, all without taking much effort or time. Before the invention of the computer, such changes would have meant hours of work in rewriting by hand. Of course, this ability to edit also has its disadvantages too (see the following section).
- *A presentational device*: Although teachers should not view the computer merely as a good way to present their students' work, there is no doubt about its importance in this aspect of written classwork. Producing a finished and beautifully presented piece of writing can be highly motivating for

children. Good presentation is also very pleasing for teachers and parents, and is useful when you want to display your students' writing. Presenting work on the computer is not just about printing out beautifully word-processed written assignments, it can also encompass the use of programs such as Powerpoint, which allow children to create a 'live' presentation of their writing.

• *Presenting worksheets*: In addition to the presentational opportunities for our children, computers also offer an excellent way for teachers to present their own worksheets. Time spent on creating engaging and exciting worksheets can be very useful in motivating your students. Because of the ease of copying and editing, a computer can also be very useful for minor differentiation of worksheets. In addition, a worksheet stored on the computer can be easily accessed, updated and printed out.

• *Help for those with SEN*: Using computers to write can be an excellent way of motivating those children who have special needs. For instance, children who find spelling very difficult can have their worries eased by the use of a spell-checker.

• *Help with technical accuracy*: Computers allow us to write with a high degree of technical accuracy. As I have said, computers should not replace the need for learning how to spell and write correctly. However, spelling- and grammar-checkers can be useful tools for identifying which words or grammatical areas the child finds difficult. Teachers and children can use these facilities to identify the areas of weakness on which they need to work.

• *Help for those with poor handwriting*: Just as the spell-checker can help the weak speller, so writing on a computer can be helpful to those who find neat or legible handwriting a challenge. Again, although the teacher clearly needs to work with these children on developing and improving their handwriting, using a computer allows them to produce and present a piece of 'finished' work, thus motivating the child.

Disadvantages

Just as we should learn to maximize the advantages of computers when working with our children on their writing, so we also need to be aware of the potential disadvantages. By being conscious of these, we can take steps to avoid the pitfalls that exist.

- *The potential for distraction*: When using a computer, it is easy to get distracted from the task in hand. For instance, there are so many different websites available on the internet, and it is so easy to click from one link to another, that a substantial amount of time can go by without anything concrete actually being achieved. Similarly, many children spend a lot of time playing with different fonts and text colours, rather than concentrating on the content of their writing. (See the section below on 'Tips for effective word-processing', pp. 183–84, for some ideas about how to overcome this problem.)
- *The potential for laziness*: Although spelling- and grammar-checkers can be very useful, there is the potential for children to use them mindlessly, without considering why and where they are making mistakes. (Again, see the 'Tips' section for ideas on how to overcome this.)
- *An easy sense of achievement*: As well as the possibility that your children may get distracted from the task in hand, computers give a sense that you have achieved something simply because it looks good. Teachers, as well as students, need to be aware that content is what really matters, no matter how beautifully presented the piece of work might be.
- *The potential for plagiarism*: Electronic encyclopaedias and, of course, the internet make it annoyingly easy for students to 'cheat' in their writing. I'm sure that many other teachers out there have also been presented with a piece of work that is blatantly plagiarized, often without the child even bothering to make any attempt to hide the original source.
- *Computers never lie*: Many of us are seduced by technology into feeling that everything we read on-screen is the 'truth'. This applies particularly to the internet – it is easy to be convinced that websites are factual and accurate, whilst this may not necessarily be true. Similarly, word-processing programs often use American spelling and grammar, and we need to be aware of this.
- *Sometimes we need to break the rules*: Carrying on from the

point above, sometimes writers will break grammatical rules on purpose, perhaps to achieve a certain tone or effect in their writing. If we rely totally on what a grammar-check tells us, we narrow down the possibilities for 'breaking the rules' and consequently for achieving some of the more interesting effects in our writing.

- *Availability of resources*: Many teachers face a situation where there are just not enough machines available, or where access to the internet is poor because of high levels of usage at certain times of the day. These factors need to be taken into account when planning ICT work. (See the section below, 'Maximizing your ICT resources', p. 186, for ways of overcoming this problem.)

- *Over-editing*: As I mentioned above, one of the most wonderful aspects of using a computer is the ability to edit without hours of rewriting by hand. However, this aspect also has its downside, in that it is often *too* easy for students to edit their work. They go on and on fiddling with the piece, long beyond the point at which they are actually improving it. With every piece of writing, there must come a point at which it is 'finished'.

- *'Typing up'*: There is always the temptation to use word-processing programs for 'typing up' handwritten pieces of work. (See the section below, 'The computer as a writing tool', pp. 184–85, for an alternative approach.)

- *The '10 per cent rule'*: The majority of us (including me) use only a fraction of what software programs actually offer us. There are many tools available of which we remain completely oblivious, probably because many of us learn 'on the job' and are not specifically trained in ICT. You may find some new ideas in the section on 'Useful word-processing functions', p. 182, below.

Potential computing hazards

The 'hazards' listed below range from the light-hearted to the potentially serious. They are all problems that I have experienced during my time as a teacher, and I do have to admit a certain admiration for the huge range of potential problems my students seem able to dream up. (I must at least pay tribute to their ingenuity.) By being aware of the problems that may occur, you should hopefully be able to prevent some of them arising.

- *Printout mania*: Many is the time that I have faced the problem of a printer with a huge quantity of print jobs backed up on it, each one a single page sent by the same student. This is the student who simply refuses to believe that (a) their work will eventually come out of the printer, or (b) one copy of their work is sufficient. To overcome this problem, explain to your children that once they have sent a page to the printer, it is stored in the printer's buffer memory. It will be printed eventually, and definitely does not need to be sent time and time again. In fact, although I advise you below to encourage your students to use the 'Ctrl' functions as a shortcut, I always insist that they use the full process with the pull-down menus when printing a document. You might also like to try insisting that your students ask permission before they send anything to print. If they refuse to go along with this, simply turn the printer off.

- *ClipArt crazy*: For children, there is apparently something magical about having pictures available to add into their work. This use of ClipArt can be problematic for a number of reasons. Firstly, pictures often take a long time to send and print out. The consequent wait can lead to a whole classful of panicking children, sending the same pages to the printer over and over again, convinced that their work is not going to appear (see 'Printout mania' above). Secondly, ClipArt pictures use up huge quantities of ink from the printer cartridge, thus making for a very expensive visit to the computer room. And thirdly, time spent fiddling around with pictures, or searching through the picture library for a suitable image, can often be at the expense of the content of the written work.

- *Crashing computers*: Considering the amount of use (and often abuse) that school computers suffer, it is surprising that they don't crash more often than they do. However, a computer crashing when a student has not saved his or her work can cause real difficulties for student and teacher. (See the section below on 'Tips for effective word-processing', pp. 183–84, for some useful advice about this problem.)

- *Internet connection problems*: Do think about possible connection problems when you plan to use the internet in your teaching, as there is nothing more frustrating than planning a lesson based on visiting various websites, only to find that your children cannot access them. The level of difficulty will vary according to the way that your school actually accesses the internet, and how the network (if there is one) is set up. The time of most difficulty seems to be mid-afternoon, when America 'logs on'.

- *Hidden windows*: The Windows operating system has a function that allows the user to have various documents and programs open at the same time, in different 'windows'. If you open a document in windows and then minimize it (a button at the top right of your screen) you will notice that it 'hides'. Keep an eye out for these hidden windows when your children are using computers. The devious amongst them may well be logging into chat-rooms or their favourite websites when you are not looking, and then minimizing these as soon as they see you coming so that they can pretend that they're working.

- *The disappearing mouse-ball*: This trick is becoming well known now, and teachers do tend to look out for it. If you have not yet experienced the disappearing mouse-ball trick, then do be aware that inside the mouse is a small ball, about the size of a gobstopper, which can be easily removed. One tip I have been given is to ask each student to turn his or her mouse upside down before they leave the room. In this way the teacher can check that all the balls are still in place.

- *Swapping the keys*: When I encountered this one I was truly amazed: in fact I didn't know whether to laugh or to cry! Basically, it is not difficult to pull the keys away from the keyboard and then swap them about. The next person to use the computer will then be thoroughly confused when their typing does not seem to be coming out as it should!

- *Fingers, fingers everywhere*: There seems to be an attraction for some children in putting their fingers into every possible area of the computer, including the CD-ROM, disk drives and electrical connections. This is not only dangerous, but is also potentially damaging to the computer. If you experience this behaviour from your students, the simple answer is to ban them from using the machines until they can treat them with the respect they deserve.

- *The big freeze*: It is worth spending some time explaining to your students what they should do if the computer crashes. The automatic reaction seems to be to turn the computer off at the mains, but if they do this the machines may become damaged. For those of you who do not already know, the best thing in these circumstances is to hit the Ctrl Alt and Delete buttons simultaneously, which will (almost always) reboot the computer. Unfortunately, a student's work will only be retained up to the point at which he or she last saved it.

- *Safety on the internet*: I have devoted a whole section to this issue below, as it is a really crucial issue for teachers to be aware of. Many of us are just beginning to see the classroom potential, both good and bad, that the internet offers. We need to develop an awareness of safety issues as soon as possible – after all, the children in our class are our responsibility. If we are going to introduce them to the world of the web, we need to ensure that they are properly equipped to deal with it.

Common word-processing errors

Writing work will generally take place using a word-processing program, and it is therefore sensible to consider some of the more common errors that your students might make. Although they are relatively simple things, the errors listed below are ones that I have seen from countless numbers of students. Rather than teaching each individual student about how to word-process correctly, it is well worth spending the first lesson or two with the whole class, going over the pitfalls to be avoided.

- *Space-bar fever*: The student with 'space-bar fever' fails to make any use of the left/right align and centre alignment functions. They also completely ignore the tab button. Over the years I have watched many students with their thumbs pressed hard down on the space bar in order to centre or right align their text. Do explain to them how simple the computer makes it for us to layout our work.

- *Wrap around*: Similarly, I have been presented with strange-looking pieces of writing, in which the student has used the return key at the end of a line, rather than allowing the text to wrap around automatically. This might not be apparent at first glance, but soon becomes a problem when the student edits the work and the new lines appear in the middle of the page.

- *New page*: In Microsoft Word, the shortcut for adding a new page is Ctrl+Return. Using this function helps prevent your students simply adding a number of returns in order to move on to a new page – a mistake that only becomes obvious when they try to change the order of their writing.

- *Blank pages*: When checking through a student's work before it is sent to print, I have often come across a series of blank pages at the end of a document. My theory is that these appear because the student overuses the return key (see above). Make sure that your students delete these blank pages before printing – otherwise you will find hundreds of clear white sheets spewing out of the printer. (Once a piece of paper has gone through the printer, it is not a good idea to reuse it.)

- *What's in a name?* The name that they give their documents might seem trivial to your students, but there is nothing more frustrating than not being able to find that masterpiece of word-processing that they spent an hour on in the last lesson. Encourage your children to find sensible and informative names for their documents. The best document names give some indication of the content of the writing, and also perhaps a hint as to who it was written by. This problem can be further overcome by getting your students to set up an individual folder on the computer in which to save their work.

Useful word-processing functions

The functions described below are all fairly basic ones, and if you are reasonably computer-literate you may wish to skip this section. Most of these functions are connected to the layout of a document, and throughout I refer to the most commonly used word-processing program, Microsoft Word (apologies to the Apple Mac users out there). I hope that you will find at least one function below that you have not yet thought about using.

- *Positioning functions*: On the toolbar towards the top of the screen there are four main options for positioning your text on the page. These are left align, centre, right align and justify. In addition, the tab button on the upper left of the keyboard is very useful for positioning words on the page. Do encourage your students not to position anything with the space bar!

- *Changing text appearance*: Just to the left of the positioning functions, there are three buttons that allow you to add bold, italic or underlining to your writing. Alternatively, you can highlight the relevant text and use the shortcuts of Ctrl+B, Ctrl+I and Ctrl+U. There are also two pull-down menus of different fonts and text sizes to the left of these buttons (in the later versions of Word these fonts are displayed as they appear on the page). In my experience, it is best to type the text first, then highlight the words that you wish to underline, change the font of, etc. On the 'Format' menu under 'Font' you will also find various different options for changing the appearance of your text, including its size, appearance, font and colour.

- *Changing the page appearance*: Adding borders to your page, or to a section of text, can make your students' writing look much more interesting (although do bear in mind the amount of printer ink these will use up). You can find this function on the pull-down menu called 'Format', under 'Borders and shading'. As well as the more straightforward borders, there is also an 'Art' section which offers some interesting alternatives. These 'Art' borders are excellent for using on worksheets.

- *Columns*: The use of columns seems to be an area of difficulty for many children, but they are extremely useful when writing in a newspaper style. You will find the function on the 'Format' menu. Do advise your students that further columns will appear automatically when they have typed to the end of the first column. When typing a newspaper article, it is a good idea to put a line between each column, to make it easier to read. This line can be added by ticking a box on the columns menu.

- *Toolbars*: On the 'View' pull-down menu, you can find a number of toolbars that are not normally displayed. These include a 'WordArt' toolbar, on which you can find some useful ready-designed WordArt titles. I would recommend that you display the 'Drawing' toolbar at all times – it includes functions for changing text and background colour, as well as arrows and other autoshapes that can prove very helpful when writing essay plans and creating other diagrams.

- *Adding symbols*: If you look at the 'Insert' pull-down menu, and then click on 'Symbol', you will find a wide range of really useful options. These 'Symbol' menus include fractions, arabic letters, copyright symbols, and so on.

Tips for effective word-processing

I am fortunate in that I worked with computers in an office environment long before I became a teacher. I was trained in how to word-process documents and also learned how to touch-type. In fact I would advise any teacher who has the time or opportunity to learn how to type properly. It makes creating worksheets a far quicker task, and is also very useful when it comes to writing computerized reports. Here, then, are a few tips that might help you and your students use the word processor more effectively when you are writing.

- *Write first, format last*: It is tempting for our students to spend vast quantities of time 'prettying up' their work as they write: changing fonts and text sizes, adding colours and shading, applying borders, and so on. However, it is always best to encourage your students to type the content first, and only then consider the presentation. There are two reasons for this. Firstly, it means that the content of the writing is done without excessive amounts of time being spent on formatting. Secondly, you might have noticed how glitches sometimes appear on the page, points at which the formatting changes for apparently no reason. For instance, if you select a new font, the computer may drop back into the default font (usually Times New Roman). This can result in very strange changes of font within a piece of writing. These glitches can be avoided by using the 'Select All' function on the 'Edit' menu, and then changing the font *after* you have finished the work.

- *Save, save, save*: I am sure that you too have had that awful experience where a child tells you 'my computer just froze/ crashed and I lost all my work'. This problem can be overcome by encouraging your children to name and save their documents right from the word go. When I am working with a class on computers, I spend the first ten minutes or so going around and checking that everyone has named and saved their work. It is also a good idea to tell your children to save their work every few minutes, as they go along (they can use Ctrl+S to do this, see below).
- *Use the 'ctrl' functions*: Microsoft Word does actually offer the user a variety of shortcuts for the most commonly used functions, such as save, bold, italic, etc. These shortcuts are, in my experience, largely ignored by students in favour of the pull-down menus at the top of the screen. However, these shortcut keys can save you a great deal of time, particularly Ctrl+S for saving a document as you go along (in fact, this should become an automatic reflex when writing on a computer). These shortcuts are listed on the pull-down menus.

The computer as a writing tool

There is a danger that we miss out on the full potential of the computer as a tool for writing. We might see it as a way for our children to 'type up' written work, or our students could set to work on a fresh piece of writing, simply starting at the beginning and stopping when they get to the end. However, computers offer us a very powerful tool for structuring, editing and working with our writing, eliminating the need for time-consuming rewriting by hand. In Chapter 6 I talked about 'building' your writing, and this is so much easier to do on a computer than on paper. Here are some ideas about how you might use the computer as an active tool, rather than simply as a passive receptor of text.

- *Outlining*: Ask your children to create an outline of their work on the computer, before they start to write. This might mean putting a series of headings, or it could be putting a single word or phrase that describes what will go into each paragraph. When writing a story, they might write a series of sentences that describe each different event or section of the story, before filling in the details.
- *Editing*: One of the most wonderful things about writing on a computer is the ability it offers to move text around with ease. Spend time getting your children familiar with the ways in which they can cut, paste and copy on the computer. These functions are at the top left of the screen, represented by the symbols of scissors (cut), paper (copy) and clipboard (paste). They can also be found on the pull-down 'Edit' menu, or can be used with the shortcuts of Ctrl+X, Ctrl+C and Ctrl+V. Your children may also need to be taught how to block their work. This can be quite a challenge for them, as it requires a reasonably high level of dexterity with the mouse. A good way of blocking single lines is to click the mouse once, with the cursor positioned just to the side of that line of text.
- *Checking technique*: Another extremely useful function of writing on a computer is the ability to check the accuracy of your work. On the 'Tools' menu you will find the function for checking spelling and grammar, or you can use the F7 button as a shortcut. Shift+F7 is also a useful shortcut for the thesaurus.

Maximizing your ICT resources

Happily, the majority of schools now have a reasonable level of ICT resources. For many schools, particularly at secondary level, this means at least one 'suite' of computers that teachers can book for their classes. However, there are still situations where a number of teachers are sharing only a few computers between their classes, or where a class of 30 students will have to make do with one machine per pair or less. In addition, many primary schools are not equipped with anything like this number of computers. Here are some thoughts about how you might maximize the resources you do have, especially if they are limited.

- *Sharing computers*: This can be a recipe for disaster unless it is well managed by the teacher. If you do need your children to work in pairs, ensure that you set the boundaries for them before this takes place. (This will help to prevent you from wasting time on settling disputes.) For instance, warn the children that they will need to take it in turns to write, and specify how this will happen. You might allow them ten minutes at a time, and then get them to swap over. You might divide the lesson time in half, for instance giving each child 30 minutes of a lesson that is one hour long. Be aware that the child who is not 'hands on' at the computer must still have a sense of involvement in the task (see below for some ideas).
- *Reader and writer*: If your children are using the computer to type up work that has already been written down by hand, one of them can act as reader while the other types the words. Approaching the activity in this way also requires them to use other skills: the reader is practising reading out loud, while the writer will have to consider how the words that they hear are spelled.
- *Typing together*: If you feel that paired sharing of computers for a specified length of time is not suitable for your children, why not ask them to type together? Depending on how slow they are, this might mean each child typing a word in turn, or perhaps a line or paragraph.
- *The computer as reward*: For many children using a computer is

a highly motivational activity – they seem to really enjoy time spent working in front of a screen, and they certainly demonstrate a high degree of concentration when they are working with ICT. This is perhaps especially true of those who do not have access to a computer at home. So, make use of the fact that the computer is viewed so positively, and if you do have limited access to machines, make them a 'reward' (at least part of the time) for those who behave or work well. Obviously, you will need to bear in mind curriculum entitlement for all, but you will generally find that all your children want to earn this so-called 'reward' and are willing to work hard to receive it.

- *Make it count*: If your access to ICT facilities is limited, make sure that the time you do spend on computers really counts. Consider how important the presentational aspects are, and whether it might be more worthwhile to use the time to practise editing and 'building' the writing.
- *Book well ahead*: There is nothing more frustrating than wanting to use a computer room but finding it booked up for months ahead. You will probably find that your school or ICT department runs a booking system for the computer rooms, and my advice would be to get in early with your booking. Halfway into a term, when the teachers are feeling like a few well-deserved lessons off, the computer room can seem remarkably appealing and any free space will be quickly snapped up!
- *Take care of the machines you do have*: With limited ICT resources, every computer counts. Spend time explaining to your children how to take care of the machines – what to do if they crash, which parts are particularly fragile and should be handled with care, and so on. For instance, the CD-ROM drive often takes a battering from negligent or poorly behaved children. Insist that they treat the school machines as they would a computer in their own home. Do look through 'Potential computing hazards' in this chapter for some more things to be wary about.

The internet in the classroom

We are really in the infancy of the use of the internet in education, and many of us are still unsure about what it offers in terms of true educational value. In addition, there are so many different websites springing up (and going out of business) that it is very time-consuming to search for those that may have something to offer us. When companies first started developing educational sites for the net, some of these were subscription-based, and schools had to pay to access them. Although there are still some of these subscription sites around, there are also many free sites now available to the teacher. Here are a few tips and thoughts about using the internet in the classroom.

- *There's no such thing as a free lunch*: Even the 'free' sites need to be funded in some way, in order to afford to run, and to produce good-quality content. There are sites out there that are not funded by advertising (see below), but do be aware that someone, somewhere is paying for the site to exist.
- *Be aware of advertising*: As teachers we need to be aware of the adverts to which we expose our children, both their number and their content. When planning work that involves using the internet, it is a good idea to check the sites first to find out how obtrusive the advertising is.
- *Find a good search engine*: A good quality search engine will save you time and effort. It will also help you find relevant content for using in specific curriculum areas. I use google (as noted earlier) as I find that it brings up good results and is straightforward to use.
- *Learn more about the 'net'*: There are some excellent books available that help make your use of the internet more effective, and which give you information about the more technical aspects of the worldwide web. I would recommend two books in particular to teachers who are using the internet in their classrooms. These are *The Internet in Schools* by Duncan Grey (London: Continuum, 2001) and Angus Kennedy's *The Rough Guide to the Internet* (London: Penguin, 2001).
- *Utilize your school website*: Many schools now have websites of

their own. If this is the case with your school, see if it is possible for you and your children to provide content for the site. Some sites are split into different departmental areas, and publishing your students' work in your own 'department' offers a highly motivational tool.

- *Set up your own website*: If your school does not have a site of its own, or if you are feeling brave, why not have a go at setting up your own website? I recently decided that I needed to set up my own author website. Before I started, I had absolutely no idea what I was doing, but I found the whole process surprisingly straightforward. There is no real need for you to be able to write (or even understand) HTML in order to create your own site. There are software programs out there that will basically do it all for you, and the moment of 'publishing' your site to the net gives a wonderful feeling of achievement. All you really need in order to write your own website is the ability to word-process a document, and perhaps a friendly colleague who has a bit of experience with ICT.

Email

The email is a very recent addition to the world of written communication. Not quite a letter, not quite a text message, the email is rapidly becoming a written form all of its own. There is quite a high level of informality in the email at present – we tend to use different vocabulary to that which we might use in a letter. The use of abbreviations (such as 'LOL') and 'emoticons' (such as ☺) is all part of this informality. In addition, correspondence between friends often does away with the need for 'proper' technique – punctuation, capital letters, paragraphing, and so on.

There is much potential in the email for teachers interested in developing literacy. To give just two ideas, many children now have access to email via a home computer. If this is the case with your students, why not email them with homework reminders, or with comments on their work and behaviour? I'm sure that receiving a message from their teacher in this way could prove highly motivational to some of them. Alternatively, you might use emails between your students in which they write a 'chain story', each adding a sentence in turn, as they receive the message.

Safety on the internet

One of the things that makes the internet such a wonderful resource is the fact that it can be used by anyone and everyone, as long as they have access to a computer with a modem. However, this also has its disadvantages, because it means that we often have no control as to whom our children might be communicating with. In addition, users of the internet are, to a large degree, 'anonymous'. It is very easy to pretend that you are someone else, and we have all heard the horror stories of children being abused via contacts made on the internet. Although there are filtering programs available, it is better to be safe than sorry, especially at this stage in the development of the technology. Here, then, are some tips about 'net safety' that you could share with your classes.

- *Keeping personal information personal*: Do warn your children about the dangers of giving out personal information on the net, particularly if they are using chat-rooms. Tell them that they should never give out their age, telephone number or address under any circumstances. If they do wish to use their real name, they should stick to using their first name only, unless they are working with their teacher via a site that links schools with each other, and that is well moderated and checked for safety.
- *Virtual people*: On the internet, we are 'virtual', we exist in cyberspace in the form that we choose to reveal. Warn your students that the people they communicate with via the internet could be anyone and anything. Many of your students will probably already be aware of this – they might be using a false persona in the chat-rooms, and other people (adults) out there will be doing the same thing. For instance it is perfectly simple for a 50-year-old man to claim that he is a fifteen-year-old boy, with all the potential abuses that might result.
- *Viruses*: We have all heard the horror stories about the different computer viruses that are swishing around the net,

but there is still a constant temptation to download. This might be opening an attachment that comes with an email we have been sent, it could be downloading a picture or program from the net. Warn your children that, with these downloads, comes the potential to infect your machines or your network.

- *Access to adult sites*: Be fully aware that when your children use the internet, it is likely that they will be able to access adult, or pornographic, sites. Even the best filtering software cannot guarantee to prevent this happening. And children being children will of course be interested to see what exciting 'adult' material they might be able to access. Keep a close eye out for any of your students who might be tempted. If you do suspect an individual, check the history log for their internet use after they have finished with the machine.

11 Celebrating writing

Let's face it, some children simply don't view writing as an exciting aspect of their lives. For the weak or the demotivated, it becomes a grind, a challenge that they must submit themselves to day after day throughout their schooling. This final chapter is about challenging that assumption: about finding ways to celebrate writing, and making it a joyful and exciting prospect. Although some of the suggestions below may take up quite a lot of your time in preparation and organization, the results in terms of motivation, behaviour and inspiration will almost always be worth the effort. The majority of the ideas below are ones that I have used or been part of during my teaching career. They stick in my mind as very positive times in my school life, and I am certain that the same applies for the children who were involved.

Publishing writing

We looked briefly at publishing children's writing in Chapter 1, and how this can help to motivate young writers. For every piece that we write, there will be an audience, or often a number of audiences. At the simplest level, the audience for the majority of classroom writing will be the teacher. There may be pieces of writing that our children produce which have a wider audience, for instance those that are put on display, or that are sent home to parents. The widest audience of all can of course be found for those pieces of work that are 'published' in some way or format. There are a wide range of ways and forms in which you might publish their work. Here are just a few ideas.

- *On the internet*: Writing that is published on the internet has a huge potential audience, and this of course includes the other children in your class or school. Having a piece of their own work published on the web will help to motivate students, and is an excellent way of celebrating their work.

- *On your classroom walls*: Although we might not really view it as 'publishing' our children's work, displaying their writing on the classroom walls is in fact a form of publication. As well as celebrating their work, displaying children's writing also helps to motivate them.

- *Via a competition*: You might run a whole-school competition, as described overleaf, and then publish the winning and commended entries in a pamphlet. This could be sold to students and parents to raise funds for your school or department, or to finance a trip or treat of some sort.

- *Via a school magazine*: If you are a keen writer and editor yourself, why not consider setting up a school magazine, if there is not already one in existence? School magazines seem to be less prevalent than they were when I was at school (perhaps because teachers are snowed under with other work). However, I can certainly remember to this day the excitement that was generated by seeing my own work published in this way.

- *Creating 'books'*: A project in which your students create their own books, from first idea to final product, would be an excellent way of celebrating their writing (not only story books, but also books in all areas of the curriculum). You might challenge your students to write a book that explains a subject to younger students, or you might ask them to write a book for their peers, perhaps on the history of your school and its local area.

Book weeks

A 'book week' is an excellent way to get the whole school celebrating reading, writing and books in general. An organization called Booktrust stages an annual book week in the UK, which takes place in the first full week of October. (You can find details of the Booktrust websites in Appendix 2 at the back of this book.) Although a book week might be organized by an English co-ordinator in the primary school, or by the English Department in a secondary school, there is no reason at all why it should not take place on a cross-curricular basis.

During book week, the focus could be on both reading and writing, perhaps with children writing their own books in the style of their favourite author. You might get local companies to sponsor your school in buying books, or ask local librarians to come in with a selection of books from the library.

Author days/weeks

A day or week dedicated to one author can be a great opportunity to get your students reading and writing in earnest. For instance, in my first school the English Department organized a Shakespeare day. Many of the teachers dressed up as characters from the plays, and performed scenes to the students. In addition, the children were involved in different writing activities, including creating Shakespearean love poems of their own. By raising the profile of a particular author in this way, you also raise the profile of writers and books in general. There is no need, of course, to stick to writers from the past. For instance, I am certain that a 'Harry Potter' day or week would go down extremely well in both primary and secondary schools.

Charity activities

Children love the chance to 'make a difference', to raise money for a cause that is close to their hearts. Many schools already take part in Red Nose Day or the Children in Need appeal. When developing charity activities for these times, consider the role that writing might play. For instance, there could be a sponsored write as well as the more typical sponsored read. The children might be allowed to 'set lines' for their teachers, and sponsor them for writing out their lines a hundred or a thousand times.

Competitions

Why not capitalize on the competitive streak that seems to run through many of our youngsters? For instance, I once set up a poetry competition that was open to the whole school. I was inundated with entries, and I published the winning and highly commended entries in a booklet. This was then sold to children and parents to help fund the prizes of book tokens. Your competition might be in a subject other than English, for instance a science competition for the best design and instructions for building a space rocket.

Writers' workshops

There are many professional writers who are able to provide workshops for schools. These might be about story-telling, poetry, writing from other cultures, and so on. In my experience, having an 'expert' come in from outside the school is very good in motivating the students with their work. You can find details of writers who provide school workshops via the internet.

'Play in a day'

It can be a wonderful experience to write alongside your students, and one way of doing this is to organize a 'Play in a day'. This could take place at the end of term, when the whole school is off timetable, for instance on an activity day. The basic format is that the teacher and students work together to produce a play in only one day, using a specified theme or the outline of a story. They could then present this play to the rest of the school, perhaps on the last day of term. The great thing about this exercise is that most of the 'writing' will take place through improvisation, and it is therefore very suitable for children who struggle with putting their thoughts down on paper.

Trips

Trips can be a great way of inspiring good writing. The children will be visiting new places, seeing new things, and will actually *want* to make a written record of their trip after the event. For instance, you might take your class to a local festival, and this could inspire some descriptive writing about what they have seen. You could take them to a museum and ask them to write about one of the exhibits. For many children, a trip is one of the most memorable and exciting events in their school career.

Part 5

Resources for Writing

Appendix 1 Text-messaging

As I have emphasized throughout this book, for us to motivate our students to write, the work that we ask them to do must be topical and interesting. And what could be more topical than text-messaging? In addition, the world of text messages gives a wonderful insight into how language develops to suit its users. So, here is a brief list of some of the more common text-message abbreviations. If you're not yet *au fait* with the world of txt msgs, you will quickly notice that many of these terms are simply the shortest possible phonic abbreviations, often using numbers such as 4 and 8 for their sounds. Alternatively, some use acronyms to replace commonly used phrases.

All the best	ATB
Are you OK?	RUOK?
Are	R
Be	B
Before	B4
Be seeing you	BCNU
Bye bye for now	BB4N
Cutie	QT
Date	D8
Easy	EZ
Excellent	XLNT
For	4
For your information	FYI
Great	GR8
Later	L8R
Laugh out loud	LOL
Oh I see	OIC
Please call me	PCM

See you later	CU L8R
Thanks	THX
To/too	2
Today	2DAY
Tomorrow	2MORO
Tonight	2NITE
Want to	WAN2
Why	Y
You	U

For further information about text-messaging, and more abbreviations, you could try:

WAN2TLK? Ltle Bk of Txt Msgs, and the accompanying series. (London: Michael O'Mara, 2000)

Or look at the following web pages:
www.bbc.co.uk/joyoftext/

www.askoxford.com/betterwriting/emoticons

This page gives a list of emoticons (email/text symbols that indicate emotion) as well as a dictionary of text-message abbreviations.

Appendix 2 Useful websites

Although it is a fantastic resource, the internet is constantly changing: each day new sites come into being, and old ones go out of commission. For this reason, please accept that some of the sites and addresses listed below may have already changed or may no longer exist. I have tried, as far as possible, to include only websites that have been running for a substantial amount of time, or which are backed up by large organizations, and are therefore more likely to remain online. I have also tried to 'weed out' the sites that subject you to those irritating pop-up adverts, or which are overly commercial.

General

www.standards.dfes.gov.uk/literacy/
Up-to-date information on literacy and the National Literacy Strategy.

www.nate.org.uk
The website of the National Association for the Teaching of English.

Writing resources

www.askoxford.com
The website of the Oxford University Press. Sections on 'The World of Words' and 'Better Writing'.

www.edufind.com/english/grammar
A very useful directory of grammatical terminology.

www.word-detective.com
The Word Detective site, which offers entertaining discussions about origin and meaning of words.

www.blewa.co.uk
A project on writing and the written word, run by the British Library.

Teaching resources

www.teachit.co.uk
A free library of English resources, useful for secondary teachers.

www.teachingideas.co.uk
An excellent resource with lots of ideas for teaching English at primary school level.

www.teachingtips.co.uk
A site for secondary teachers, run by Longman Pearson.

Story-writing

www.the-phone-book.com
A showcase for short and ultra-short stories written for mobile phones.

Publishing your children's writing

www.thescriptorium.net
A great site run by Sherry Ramsey, a Canadian writer. There is a special section for young writers called 'Scriptorium Scribbles'.

www.kidsnews.com
This site publishes a wide range of children's writing from around the world.

Children's books

www.booktrust.org.uk
The site of the Book Trust, which runs the National Children's book week.

www.booktrusted.com
A second Book Trust site, dedicated to children's literature.

www.terry-deary.com
A fun site from the author of the *Horrible Histories*, with interesting graphics and some spooky audio. Terry can be emailed via the site.

www.annefine.co.uk
The website of the new Children's Laureate. It is not possible to email Anne Fine via the site.

Writing to penpals

When using the internet to communicate with schools and students around the world, teachers do need to be aware of the safety issues involved. I would strongly recommend that you talk to your children about sensible behaviour on the internet. You can find more information about this in Chapter 10.

www.epals.com
An excellent site, with clear design and a strong international focus. Strongly safety-conscious.

www.teaching.com/keypals
A clear site, with unobtrusive advertising.

www.agirlsworld.com/penpal/index.html
A colourful, fun site, but only for girls, and with quite an American slant.

www.interpals.net
This site offers penpals via email, but it does have some advertising and pop-ups.

Special educational needs

www.dyslexia-inst.org.uk
The website of the Dyslexia Institute.

www.bda-dyslexia.org.uk
The website of the British Dyslexia Association.

Appendix 3 Vocabulary

The lists in this appendix provide some useful vocabulary for written work in a variety of subject areas. You might like to use them to introduce key terms, or to set spelling tests for your students. I have included a list of some of the most commonly used words, which will be useful for teaching and consolidating vocabulary at both primary and secondary level. I have also included a list of words that, in my experience, cause particular problems for older students.

Commonly used words

a, about, across, after, again, all, almost, among, an, and, any, as, at, be, because, before, between, by, come, do, down, enough, even, ever, every, far, for, forward, from, get, give, go, have, he, hear, here, how, I, if, in, keep, let, little, make, may, me, much, near, no, not, now, of, off, on, only, or, other, our, out, over, please, put, quite, said, say, see, seem, send, she, so, some, still, such, take, than, that, the, then, there, this, though, through, to, together, tomorrow, under, up, very, well, when, where, while, who, why, will, with, yes, yesterday, you, your

Commonly used nouns

ant, apple, arm, baby, bag, ball, band, basket, bath, bed, bee, bell, bird, board, boat, book, boot, bottle, box, boy, branch, brick, bridge, brush, bucket, button, cake, camera, card, cart, cat, chain, cheese, chin, church, circle, clock, cloud, coat, collar, cow, cup, curtain, cushion, dog, door, drawer, dress, ear, egg, engine, eye, face, farm, feather, finger, fish, flag, floor, fly, foot, fork, garden, girl, glove, hair, hand, hat, head, heart, horse, hospital, house, island, jewel, kettle, key, knee, knife, leaf, leg, library, line, lip, lock, map, match, monkey, moon, mouth, nail, neck, needle, net, nose, nut, office, orange, oven, parcel, pen, pencil, picture, pig, pin, plane, plate, pocket, pot, potato, rail, rat, ring, roof, root, sail, school, scissors, sheep, shelf, ship, shirt, shoe, skirt, snake, sock, spade, spoon, square, stamp, star, station, stick, stomach, street, sun, table, tail, thumb, ticket, toe, tooth, town, train, tree, trousers, umbrella, wall, watch, wheel, window, wing, worm

Problem words for older students
accommodation, beautiful, beginning, cautious, competition, definitely, desperate, disguise, exaggerate, explanation, extraordinary, February, frightened, laughter, occasion, opinion, particularly, patiently, prejudice, privilege, separate, successfully, suspicious

English

Linguistic analysis
alliteration, atmosphere, cliché, comparison, expression, figurative, imagery, metaphor, onomatopoeia, personification, simile

Spelling, punctuation and grammar
apostrophe, clause, comma, conjunction, consonant, exclamation, homonym, paragraph, plural, prefix, preposition, subordinate, suffix, synonym, vocabulary, vowel

Writing about texts
advertise, advertisement, chorus, climax, dialogue, genre, myth, narrative, narrator, opinion, pamphlet, playwright, rehearse, resolution, rhyme, scene, significant, soliloquy, tabloid

Writing about characters

ambitious, cautious, character, characterisation, courageous, despised, disguise, enemies, foolish, hypocritical, notorious, obedient, rebellious, relationship, serious, vicious

Letter-writing

apologise, complain, enquire, faithfully, forward, information, madam, receive, sincerely, writing

Science

absorb, acid, alkaline, apparatus, chemical, circulation, condensation, digestion, dissolve, distil, element, evaporation, friction, function, growth, hazard, laboratory, liquid, mammal, nutrient, organism, oxygen, particles, reproduce, respiration, solution, temperature, thermometer, vertebrate, vessel

Maths

addition, angle, amount, approximately, average, calculate, centimetre, circumference, decimal, diameter, division, equilateral, fraction, graph, horizontal, kilogram, metre, minus, multiplication, quadrilateral, radius, rectangle, square, subtraction, symmetrical, triangle, vertical, weight

History

agricultural, castle, chronological, civilisation, colonisation, defence, disease, document, dynasty, emigration, government, immigrant, independence, invasion, parliament, political, propaganda, rebel, rebellion, reign, republic, revolution, siege, traitor

Geography

abroad, atlas, climate, country, county, employment, erosion, estuary, globe, habitat, infrastructure, international, landscape, latitude, longitude, national, physical, pollution, poverty, regional, rural, settlement, tourism, transportation, urban, weather

RE

baptism, Bible, biblical, Buddhism, Buddhist, celebration, ceremony, Christian, commandment, creation, disciple, faith, festival, Hindu, Hinduism, hymn, Islam, Islamic, Jewish, Judaism, miracle, morality, Muslim, parable, pilgrimage, prayer, prophet, religion, religious, shrine, Sikh, Sikhism, spiritual, symbol, synagogue, temple, worship

Appendix 4 Marking Symbols

~ ~ ~	Expression/grammar is incorrect
_____	Spelling mistake/word is wrong
//	Insert paragraph
^	Word missing/insert word or letter
O	Punctuation missing
?	Unclear/don't understand what is meant
/.	Cut letter/punctuation
✓	Good section
✓✓	Excellent section

Index